PRAISE FOR NI
SCALED, AND AGILE

"This book provides a timely and insightful lens for thoughtful discourse on designing organizations in our fast-changing landscape. Its focus on networks, scale, and agility deeply resonate with our efforts in the Singapore Public Service to design the future of work, workplace, and workforce in our agencies."
Ong Toon Hui, Dean and CEO, Civil Service College, Singapore

"Kates, Kesler, and DiMartino build on well-tested theories of human behavior and large-scale systems to show how organization design frameworks apply to the new and challenging realities of today."
Charles Snow, Professor Emeritus, Penn State Smeal College of Business

"This is the perfect book for leaders who need to align their organization with the strategy, and who are searching for a comprehensive framework. Kates, Kesler, and DiMartino discuss the design of the overall operating model, horizontal linkages, as well as the vertical layers and roles in complex organizations. They also provide numerous practical examples of how we can design organization to achieve both agility and efficiency."
Nicolay Worren, Associate Professor, School of Economics and Business, Norwegian University of Life Sciences, Co-founder of Reconfig, Member of the curatorial board of the European Organization Design Forum

Networked, Scaled, and Agile

A Design Strategy for
Complex Organizations

Amy Kates
Greg Kesler
Michele DiMartino

Publisher's note

Every possible effort has been made to ensure that the information contained in this book is accurate at the time of going to press, and the publishers and authors cannot accept responsibility for any errors or omissions, however caused. No responsibility for loss or damage occasioned to any person acting, or refraining from action, as a result of the material in this publication can be accepted by the publisher or the authors.

First published in Great Britain and the United States in 2021 by Kogan Page Limited

2nd Floor, 45 Gee Street	122 W 27th St, 10th Floor	4737/23 Ansari Road
London	New York, NY 10001	Daryaganj
EC1V 3RS	USA	New Delhi 110002
United Kingdom		India

www.koganpage.com

Kogan Page books are printed on paper from sustainable forests.

ISBNs

Hardback	978 1 78966 781 3
Paperback	978 1 78966 779 0
Ebook	978 1 78966 780 6

Library of Congress Control Number

2021930676

British Library Cataloguing-in-Publication Data

A CIP record for this book is available from the British Library.

Typeset by Integra Software Services, Pondicherry
Print production managed by Jellyfish
Printed and bound by CPI Group (UK) Ltd, Croydon CR0 4YY

To the team that built our firm:

Rollin Burhans, Tom Falkowski, Julia Law, Karen Duvall, Tom Jasinski, Jaclyn Kates, Cynthia Escamilla, Jonathan Hornyak, Laurie Gerontianos, Blake Bowersock, and Darko Lovric

CONTENTS

LIST OF FIGURES
AND TABLES

Figures

Tables

ABOUT THE AUTHORS

Amy Kates is an organization designer consulting to leaders of corporations, non-profits, and governments around the world. She teaches at Cornell University and is the co-author of four other books on organization design. The methodology developed with her colleagues has become a standard in the field. She is a co-founder of Kates Kesler Organization Consulting and is currently a Managing Director at Accenture.

Greg Kesler consults with CEOs in the design of global operating models. He specializes in aligning organizations around new business models and complex strategies. He is the co-author of two other books in the field. He is co-founder of Kates Kesler Organization Consulting and is currently a Managing Director at Accenture.

Michele DiMartino consults with CEOs and executive teams on the design and activation of their company operating models. She specializes in working with senior leadership groups to co-create new organizations, while helping them become stronger as a team. She is also an organization design instructor for Kates Kesler and guest lecturer at Cornell University and New York University. Michele is a Kates Kesler Organization Consulting partner and a Managing Director at Accenture.

FOREWORD

We are in an unparalleled time of change. We believed 2020 would begin a decade of transformation in every industry and in every company through digital and technology that would mean new ways of working, new ways of making decisions, and new ways of engaging with each other and with customers. The Covid-19 crisis accelerated this transformation, making it clear that companies would need to achieve digital transformation of their entire enterprise much faster. As we close 2020, we are at the beginning of what we think is a once-in-an-era, massive re-platforming of global business over the next five years.

Today's CEOs have two clear imperatives. One is to transform every aspect of the enterprise using digital and technology to realize value. The other is to move at unprecedented speed and scale, especially for large organizations, while bringing their people along the journey.

Addressing these imperatives demands answering age-old questions about how to break down internal silos and build horizontal networks. While these challenges are not new, they are inseparable from success. To achieve these imperatives, you must have an organizational design that creates the right connections and the right conversations, led by the right leaders.

At Accenture, we learned that lesson in 2014 as we began transforming our company to be a leader in digital, cloud, and security services. We put in a growth model of our own organizational design that moved those services from less than 20 percent of our business to more than 70 percent today. As we completed that strategy in 2019, we set our sights on our next transformation—capturing the opportunities created by this strong platform of capabilities and the market momentum around digital and technology-enabled transformation. We knew our first priority was finding the right organizational design.

I was a new CEO on September 1, 2019, and I wanted to put the new growth model in place on March 1, 2020. The ambition was to move faster than we had ever seen any organization of our scale move. Imagine a $43 billion company with more than 500,000 people designing and implementing—within six months—a new growth model that would evolve our services, the way we operate, our leadership, and our culture. This included changing our P&L in the middle of our fiscal year, eliminating 32 percent of our management nodes, and changing the role of roughly 200 of our top 300 leaders in a single day. And we needed to do so without disrupting the strong momentum we had in the market.

To get the organizational design right, I turned to some of the strongest leaders in the field—Greg, Amy, and Michele at Kates Kesler Organizational Consulting. Within weeks, it became apparent that not only would the Kates Kesler team be critical to achieving our goal, but also their specialized skills, which transformations demand, would be an increasing need for our clients. They are now part of Accenture.

The team brought fresh perspective and a deep knowledge of organization. They asked the right questions and guided work streams that would bring to life our organization's focus on shared success with our clients, our people, our shareholders, our partners, and our communities. The scale and speed at which we worked were extraordinary and a true example of what agile really means. On March 1, 2020, we implemented our new growth model, which included simplifying our organizational structure and new ways of working with each other. We did so having delivered the strongest sales quarter in our history, with outstanding revenue growth.

Like most companies on transformational journeys, one of our greatest organizational challenges was building those horizontal networks while focusing on how to work across our services and markets to deliver end-to-end solutions to our clients as a responsible business. To succeed, it's about having the right conversations with the right people. Continuously.

It is worth noting how Kates Kesler works and how they fit into our transformation. A new organizational design was not the goal, but rather was a key enabler to the transformation we were seeking. Kates Kesler joined our team, quickly got up to speed on our strategic goals, asked the right, hard questions, and gained the trust of very senior executives. Imagine being a consultant to a group of consultants! They pushed us to have the difficult conversations—remember, we eliminated nearly a third of our management nodes. They worked seamlessly with the broader team, and in particular, our change management team. We were using our transformation as a testing ground for new, state-of-the-art change management techniques to enable faster change and adoption, and they were a great thought partner.

What was particularly striking to me was the first meeting our Chief Leadership and Human Resources Officer, Ellyn Shook, and I had with them. They were clear: They could not be effective, and we could not achieve the, frankly, unheard of speed from design to implementation unless I was directly involved. And they would not do the work without that commitment. I immediately trusted them because they were direct and unambiguous.

The people-focused design features and insights the authors have gained from working with scores of large global companies, through similar issues, are the focus of this new book from the Kates Kesler team. It is a timely strategy for building organizations suited to the opportunities that today's business model and technology innovation demand.

Julie Sweet
CEO, Accenture

The Central Design Problem

In 2018 IBM paid $34 billion to buy the open-source software leader, Red Hat. Eyebrows were raised among all who were watching the enterprise technology sector. The largest software company acquisition ever—for what? It certainly was not the revenue stream from the Linux-based products. The explanation for the deal was that IBM was buying an extraordinary team of very talented people. The only problem with that theory, of course, is that people can walk. The business press quickly observed that the success of the deal would depend on how well IBM managed the integration. In simple terms, how willing would Big Blue be to keep its hands off the Red Hat culture while finding ways to connect it into the existing business?

IBM's bet is focused on a future paradigm for enterprise IT called hybrid cloud. The business case is based on the prediction that companies will seek blended public and private cloud infrastructure, to combine with their legacy hardware. Red Hat provides critical capabilities as well as the credibility to make IBM a player in that market. For this gamble to work, the Red Hat assets must be separate, and, at the same time, they must become part of the larger company. Red Hat must remain platform-neutral with its legacy clients. But elements of its go-to-market model need to be integrated into IBM in order to extend Red Hat's opportunities with IBM's sales and marketing reach.

Then there is the matter of culture, or more accurately, cultures. In Red Hat, everyone is an "associate," while IBM's adherence to hierarchy remains mostly intact. Red Hat norms are cult-like, similar to those in other successful start-ups, centered on a purpose or a cause—not just open source, but making the world a better place by encouraging all users to be part of making the product better. IBM has long focused on discipline, planning, and making the numbers. Some have argued that the play should be to move the Red Hat culture to IBM. The appointment of Red Hat's CEO in early 2020 to the position of chief operating officer of IBM appeared to be a step in that direction.

This kind of organizational tension is inherent whenever a business changes its portfolio, whether organically or through acquisition. The new always challenges the old. And, as every industry reshapes as a result of the economic impacts of Covid-19, seeing and addressing these tensions becomes even more important. A number of health insurance companies in the United States are buying pharmacy benefit managers. While the potential synergies are clear, the advantages of scale and market reach have to be balanced with the need to maintain separation and neutrality with legacy pharmacy clients. These clients are healthcare benefit payers who use the pharmacy provider, a competitor of health insurance company. The new and more complex business model will need to change, and the offering will be built in at least two forms: a) integrated health services, which will be a bundled solution; and b) a more narrowly focused pharmacy service for clients who wish to retain their existing health insurance provider. Integrated with some clients; separated from others.

Red Hat CEO Jim Whitehurst asserted on the day of the announced acquisition by IBM that "Red Hat is still Red Hat and the company will function as a distinct unit within IBM" (Ohnesorge, 2019). That assertion may change over time. It is the rare organization today that doesn't need to integrate in some way. IBM/Red Hat and Cigna/Express Scripts are dramatic examples of the need to design organizations to bring the benefits of being big and being small at the same time. The puzzle of how to balance the benefits of scale and integration with the benefits of separation and focus can only be solved through sophisticated organizational arrangements.

As we move into a new and more complicated decade, a similar dynamic plays out in many of our clients and the companies we watch closely. We have found a historic metaphor helps illustrate this critical organizational problem of the 2020s.

The Square and the Tower

The history of the world is largely the story of a central tension that has played out for millennia in what historian Niall Ferguson (2018) characterized as "the square and the tower." Throughout history the tower has represented reigning authority and hierarchy. The square is the community of people that naturally form to resist hierarchy—networks that conspire against the tower.

From Luther and the Reformation in Europe 500 years ago seeking to remake the Catholic Church, to the Bolshevik Revolution in the early 19th century, to the 2010s Arab Spring that began in Egypt on Facebook, networks have sought to bring down authority in the tower and the concentrated power it represents. For most of history, the tower has overshadowed the square because the history of humanity is largely about military conquest and building defenses, and these require command and control. Those "towers" in Western and Eastern cultures established organizations capable of building great walls, pyramids, roads across continents, and powerful city-states.

There is an inherent and healthy tension between the tower and the square, between hierarchy and networks. When power is absolute and sits in one place for too long, the square must resist. But looking across the centuries, the two have co-existed and mostly to the benefit of humanity, argues Ferguson.

Fast forward to 2020. The belief of the past 30 years that we were headed toward a "single global market" now seems naïve. Britain's assault on the Eurozone and America's populist turn toward tariffs both feel like a rebellion in the square, pushing back on elites in the tower. Global corporations have had to adjust, often realigning their organizations toward more decentralized, locally oriented organizations, sometimes only a few years after having built highly centralized, global business units. And others are realigning their operating models to scale their brands and technologies globally, eliminating duplication among decentralized profit and loss units. The Coronavirus exposed the fragility of supply chains that have products moving across multiple national boundaries.

Business models are changing at an unprecedented rate, powered by technology, with converging forces across the value chain. As AI is fully woven into the customer-facing parts of the business, companies must change the way they operate. The lines between industries blur as algorithms decide how to assign Uber drivers to riders, how to price products online, and how to forecast and schedule production. The Conference Board survey in 2020 called out "creating new business models" as the second greatest concern CEOs have for their companies (The Conference Board, 2020).

These new business models shift power inside the company. The launch of Disney+ transforms Disney's place in the industry while also disrupting its own historic business model. In the organization, power is shifting in Disney from the movie studios and regional distribution companies to a global direct-to-consumer "tower."

In contrast, Royal Dutch Philips has nearly completed its transformation into a healthcare technology company, in which its imaging-systems hardware is only one component in a solution bundle that includes software and business and health services. Global product managers have handed authority over to general managers in the local markets who bundle hardware, software, and services components into customized health-system solutions that fit the varied needs of their regional customers. In Philips, the global "tower" has given way to the market "square."

Nike is now a full-force retailer, as well as wholesaler, with stunning gains in its online as well as its brick-and-mortar sales channels. In Nike the square and the tower have co-existed for nearly a decade in a carefully engineered balance that governs how much of its seasonal apparel and footwear collection will be the same around the world and how much will be unique to regional markets. The results have been exceptional in the otherwise sleepy apparel and retail businesses. Nike has mastered an organization that can be big and small at the same time.

In addition, a whole new set of expectations has emerged for top leaders in today's large, publicly held corporations. Along with having to deal with the tension between globalism and nationalism, trade wars, AI, digital business, and cybersecurity, top executives are increasingly expected to take stands on a number of social issues and meet new standards of safety in expectation of the next pandemic. Today, they must balance the demands of multiple stakeholder groups who are calling for change in everything from a sustainable climate policy to income inequality. Retired PepsiCo CEO Indra Nooyi recently asserted, "There is a leadership vacuum today that CEOs are expected to step into and fill, because others are failing at the job" (Stoll, 2019). Those "others" include politicians in Eastern and Western countries alike. Blackrock CEO Larry Fink was making a practical business assessment when he told the CEOs of the firms his company invests $7 trillion in that "our investment conviction is that sustainability- and climate-integrated portfolios can provide better risk-adjusted returns to investors. And with the impact of sustainability on investment returns increasing, we believe that sustainable investing is the strongest foundation for client portfolios going forward" (Fink, 2020). If Nooyi and Fink are right, then corporations will bear a greater burden in attending to a broader community of stakeholders in the coming decade. This will only make organizations more complex systems to design and manage.

Core Tensions in Complex Organizations

The tension between the tower and the square takes many forms in today's complex organization. In your company, you may see it as a pull between local and enterprise agility, autonomy and scale, global and local, core business profitability and start-up energy, or speed and leverage. Today, the term "agility" is often used to mean differentiation (small, autonomous, local), while "scale" refers to the benefits of integration (big, connected, global) as shown in Figure 1.1.

The balance of power across these polarities not only will be unique for each company but also will need to shift ahead of or in response to changes in the environment. Let's examine some of these tensions.

When "agile" is used in its common form, we tend to think of small and separate business units that move quickly and locally. While this seems an appealing outcome, these models are also prone to duplicated resources, overemphasis on differences, and lack of connection and leverage. Another kind of agility is "enterprise agility"—the ability of the entire company to make fast adjustments regarding where to invest in markets, innovation, technology, and talent. Apple has always been an example of enterprise agility, betting big on new ideas and putting the resources of the organization behind them.

Figure 1.1 Differentiated vs integrated

Agile: Differentiated, Local	Scaled: Integrated, Global
• Locally responsive to differences • Focused on customers, product, regions • Vertical business units • Clear accountability for profit and loss (P&L)	• Fewer, bigger bets • Movement of talent, ideas, innovation • Shared resourcing and services • Global reach

 Differentiated
Adapt to market variations
Business unit speed
Autonomous decision-making

 Integrated
Adapt to new enterprise priorities
Enterprise speed, portfolio shifts
Harmonized, consolidated

 Duplicated resources
P&L complexity
High cost, lower return on assets

 Bureaucratic
Distance from customer
Less accountability

Both forms of agility—local and enterprise—matter in the 21st century, and the tension can be productive. The essential role of leaders is to find the right balance in order to gain the benefits of small, divisional, local units as well as the benefits of large, integrated organizations that exploit the collective assets of scale. In a truly collaborative organization, the tower and the square are both valued. Hierarchy and networks co-exist to deliver the value that shareholders expect from large companies.

Being small and big at the same time increasingly means carving out focused organizations that can create disruptive innovation—often disruptive to one's own business as well as others. The late Clayton Christensen (1997) called the disruption of one's own business model as the inevitable effect of true innovation the "innovator's dilemma." The organization must be designed to accommodate today's scaled profit engine as well as the agility of tomorrow's fledgling businesses. Mailchimp, a US-focused online marketing and sales services firm, is building an integrated marketing platform that brings comprehensive solutions to its small-business customers. It must organize to continue to grow its legacy email marketing business while scaling up the new platform.

These tensions between big and small, and integration versus differentiation, are nothing new to organization designers (Lawrence and Lorsch, 1967). Galbraith (2010) foresaw the need for organizations to become more "reconfigurable" years ago. The power of the reconfigurable organization is that leaders can move work to where talent, capabilities, and capacity are, regardless of where those resources are located in the world.

The Challenge of Being Global in the 2020s

This brings us to the unique challenges of global organizations. That the possibility of designing global, multi-dimensional organizations that can move fast exists does not mean it is easy. The tension between global and local is a familiar organization design problem. In the 1980s, Bartlett and Ghoshal (1989) laid out the fundamental dilemma facing multinational firms: how to achieve global coordination while simultaneously being able to be locally responsive. All organizations—even the digital natives built for speed from the ground up—face challenges of making decisions and organizing work across boundaries.

Historically, product and services companies have chosen to grow across national borders by replicating their success formula and delivering it in the local context (Galbraith, 2000). In this model, general managers are empowered to start with sales and marketing organizations and then invest in operational infrastructure. These "local-for-local" approaches are effective market-entry strategies, but often prove expensive to operate for the long term. Even enterprise leaders firmly committed to decentralized philosophies soon find that they cannot sustain the complexity and costs of atomized market units led by mini-CEOs.

In the 2000s, we saw the pendulum swing the other way. Technology advances led many business leaders to buy into "the world is flat" rhetoric and predictions that global tastes and needs would converge. They dialed back autonomy and decision authority from country-based teams and transferred those powers to global product groups. Many went too far, however, in centralizing and consolidating global product and brand management. As a result, they soon found themselves under attack by nimble, local competitors.

Beginning in the 2010s, we started to see a new flavor of global. Even digital companies need to localize their products, but no longer is the same infrastructure needed as in the past. When Spotify and Google move their success formula across borders, they can move into new markets without moving a lot of people. Global footprint strategies are today more about how best to optimize talent costs for research, development, and operations work.

The food-and-beverage industry provides a good example of this tension. While the PepsiCo brand is global, products in the company's expansive portfolio are highly adapted to local markets. Ingredients, flavor profiles, packaging, consumer marketing, and retail relationships must all be tailored to local tastes. Market leaders need, and are given, high degrees of authority so that they can compete in a fast-moving, low-margin business. At the same time, PepsiCo gains advantage over local players by leveraging deep expertise in food-science research and global consumer insights data. Its functional infrastructure, such as human resources and finance systems, is highly consolidated. PepsiCo builds these capabilities through strong coordination at the enterprise level while empowering geographic leaders to be very entrepreneurial in product creation and marketing execution.

Or, consider Otis Elevator, a 170-year-old industry leader that has installed its elevators in the Empire State Building, the Eiffel Tower, and the Burj Khalifa. Otis, headquartered in Connecticut in the US, has grown successfully with strong regional centers of power. Leaders pride themselves in being viewed as a "French company" in France. This is strategically useful. Variations among North American, European, and Asian building standards, construction methods, and economics continue to make it necessary to tailor technologies and product designs to real market differences.

But today, Otis also needs to incorporate sophisticated digital technologies to enable dynamic capacity management in 100-story towers, improve returns on new equipment installations, and meet complex demands from customers for internet-of-things-enabled services. More global harmonization of design and production has become critical. But a single global elevator design is simply not realistic across North America, Europe, and East Asia, so Otis had to find an organizational model that could deliver both global scale and local agility. Its 2020 organization enables the company to build common product and service platforms that can be adapted to regional variations in a profitable, customer-focused manner, competing against both global and local players who are willing to go to market at lower price points.

The current wave in global organization design avoids the simplistic dichotomies of central versus decentral management structures. Today's successful global organization must be simultaneously built to be global and local (Kesler and Kates, 2016).

Scale: The Benefits of Thinking Big

There is a simple reality in micro-economics that eventually comes to bear on even the smallest and most innovative start-up. As entities grow, economies of scale can provide competitive advantages by reducing per-unit costs. While some companies foolishly over-prioritize these benefits, as is often apparent in the merger of two companies that otherwise gain no real synergies, scale does often matter. In cost-focused organization designs, consolidating operations plays out in many familiar ways, notably, production and supply chain collaboration, promotion and costs of selling, administrative headquarters efficiency, and the like. Even in services and software, where the product is exponentially scalable without further capital investment, scale of specialization of talent or user networks quickly becomes a differentiator.

But there are innovation- and growth-oriented benefits of scale and integration as well. VF Corporation is a global apparel company with familiar brands such as Timberland, Vans, and The North Face. CEO Steve Rendle had watched as each region in the world created its own marketing stories, developed its own products, and created its own retail experience for consumers for many of the brands. At the same time, it was apparent that VF's quirky but powerful Vans footwear and apparel brand worked in a much more transnational manner, and with a much greater growth trajectory. Its SoCal skateboarding culture had transplanted to China surprisingly well.

When brand stories and ethos (what the brand stands for) can be harmonized across geographies and cultures, the result is a more powerful "customer promise" that can command greater sales, higher prices, and loyalty. Global brands enable more globally consistent product, which can deliver enormous productivity gains across the value stream. Apple and Nike are clear cases in point. This kind of scale is less about cost reduction and more about value creation.

In VF Corporation, the global Vans organization had already moved to a more global organization model than the other big brands, and it served as a model for the future of the larger company. Vans had managed to build a very tight global community. The collaborative processes and forums already at work inside this trendy brand served as inspiration for realigning the other brand and regional commercial units across VF. Investments in product and brand innovation became more transnational, focused on fewer, bigger ideas.

Scale is created by bringing the best of what the tower has to offer in terms of connections across boundaries with a holistic view of the broader enterprise. When leaders use the words integration, whole, global, leveraged, center-led, and power-of-one in their strategies, then one can safely predict they will be followed by organization changes designed to gain the benefits of scale.

Agility: The Benefits of Acting Small

Agility is a much more challenging concept, and a term that is used in so many contexts in business today that it almost has no meaning. Agile methodology, originally focused on software product development, is a well-defined specific discipline and set of practices for managing complex programs that rely on small teams, led by product managers who connect the work of the development team to the user, translating requirements into technical specifications and project plans. It features short bursts of iteration with quick releases of product and immediate feedback. Teams are empowered to set their own schedules within broad frameworks. At its essence, Agile is a disciplined and rigorous way to run cross-functional work teams. The prevalence of technology companies and the need for almost every company to develop some software internally has spread Agile, and related practices, widely. At Siemens, Netflix, Amazon and others, Agile teams have long been incorporated into the way they define the customer experience, and approaches to developing new products. PepsiCo and other more conventional companies are actively experimenting with functional teams attempting to use Agile to innovate human resources and other management practices.

Increasingly, companies are seeking to scale Agile teams across the entire organization. Some have argued for a clear distinction between scaling the model by adding hundreds of agile teams, versus clean-sheet design for an "agile organization" (Rigby et al, 2020) This is an important principle that challenges us to think about the core operating model of the company with a clear definition of the *problem we are trying to solve*, rather than chasing shiny objects.

Some companies are realigning their corporate operating models by adopting an Agile-scaling framework, selected from among a number of emerging models. These frameworks have been branded, to a degree, by zealots who espouse their benefits, and there is no research or even expansive reporting that argues one is better than the other. Companies like ING and Bosch in Europe, Haier in China, and Home Depot in the US have famously built on the organizational thinking pioneered at Spotify that connects scores or even hundreds of Agile teams into networks and teams of teams, and rethinks the roles of the top leadership teams to incorporate agile thinking into their operating models.

To be sure, large companies with multi-dimensional strategies and lines of business will not find that adopting Agile team methods always makes the organization more effective. When you have multiple products delivered to serve multiple client segments around the world, you need to find a way to both leverage your resources and move fast. Organizational agility means being able to easily form a team-of-teams across a global network. This agility only comes through the thoughtful design of vertical, as well as horizontal structures, governance forums and practices, and clear decision rights. The ability to set and communicate *strategy* (choosing what to do and not do) and *priorities* (setting a sequence of activity) requires a high degree of coordination across leadership. It is a team process, but one that must be held at the senior levels.

We are encouraged by the level of experimentation, but believe design should not follow fashion, and clear definition of a given company's design purpose is critical. (Spotify leadership have long argued that other companies should not attempt to copy their model.) We hope to contribute to the conversation with this book, although Agile itself is not our focus.

Most conflicts in the organization design process arise from differences in perspective. When any business or organization challenge is examined from the perspective of an operating unit leader, that leader will often emphasize the need for more differentiation and focus. A typical response is, "If you want me to succeed, give me control over the resources and decisions that will allow me to move fast and autonomously."

But, viewed from the perspective of the enterprise, organizing around several autonomous geographic or product-oriented profit and loss centers often creates predictable barriers to enterprise agility (Sull, 2009). These units tend to produce smaller innovations that, taken together, do not really move the meter for the company as a whole. In the case of a $20 billion provider of renal-patient care that is trying to bring an integrated, value-based solution to the market, its separate business units focused on equipment sales, dialysis centers, and disposable devices, all represent a set of silos that the sales team must battle every time they attempt to negotiate a contract for an integrated offering for a health care provider or payer. Examples abound of the crippling effects of "agile business units" that cannot work together to deliver a complete customer experience at the enterprise level. Agile teams can be embedded in the organization, but if the operating model, its management processes, and its technology backbone do not create an agile environment, empowered teams on their own are not likely to add up to an agile organization.

When leaders use the word "agile" it is often code for separate, differentiated, focused, autonomous, local, or decentralized. One must confirm if the goal is speed and responsiveness at an operating unit level or at an enterprise level.

Networked, Scaled, and Agile

Our clients know that it is not an option to choose between agility and scale. CEOs want to know how to:

- move fast in the market while leveraging corporate assets
- run a global brand while delivering it with local relevance
- build common platforms while accommodating regulatory and technology differences across geographic boundaries.

Once the right balance is found between differentiation and integration, then linking the parts through structured, well-designed networks becomes the way to move assets, ideas, and talent across borders and boundaries. The only way to design an organization that can uniquely gain the benefits of all the tensions in a strategy is through a systemic approach. Jay Galbraith's Star Model (Figure 1.2) remains the best way to shape human behavior at the organizational level.

The Star Model gives us the levers to adjust when creating a system of organization behavior and business outcomes. But it does not tell us how to make the trade-offs between options for a given strategy. The remainder of this book provides the frameworks and tools for making decisions that will create the right mix of networked, scaled, and agile for your organization.

Figure 1.2 The Star Model

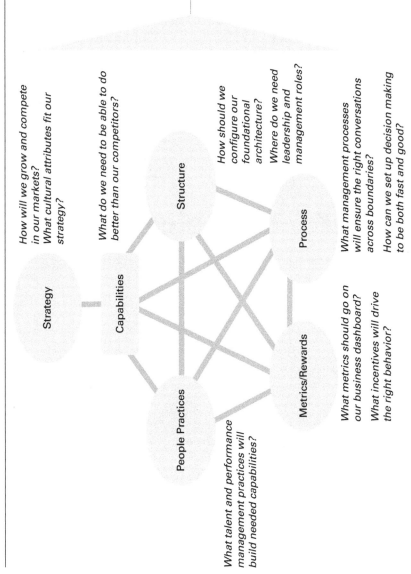

How will we grow and compete in our markets?
What cultural attributes fit our strategy?

What do we need to be able to do better than our competitors?

How should we configure our foundational architecture?

Where do we need leadership and management roles?

What management processes will ensure the right conversations across boundaries?

How can we set up decision making to be both fast and good?

What metrics should go on our business dashboard?
What incentives will drive the right behavior?

What talent and performance management practices will build needed capabilities?

Strategy

Capabilities

Structure

Process

Metrics/Rewards

People Practices

Culture, Performance, Results

ALIGNMENT = EFFECTIVENESS

SOURCE Galbraith (1995)

Key Takeaways

- Organizations reflect the tensions that have characterized human history for hundreds of years between vertical power (tower) and horizontal power (square).

- Purposeful organization design creates the right balance between local and enterprise agility, autonomy and scale, global and local perspectives, core business profitability and start-up energy, and speed and leverage that is right for the company's strategy and context.

- It is possible to get the benefits of scale and agility using structured networks and a Star Model based system design approach.

References

Bartlett, C A and Ghoshal, S (1989) *Managing Across Borders: The transnational solution*, Harvard Business Review Press, Brighton, MA

Christensen, C M (1997) *The Innovator's Dilemma*, Harvard Business Review Press, Brighton, MA

Ferguson, N (2018) *The Square and the Tower: Networks and power, from the Freemasons to Facebook*, Penguin Books, New York

Fink, L (2020) A fundamental reshaping of finance, Black Rock. www.blackrock.com/corporate/investor-relations/larry-fink-ceo-letter (archived at https://perma.cc/7X96-FW8Z)

Galbraith, J R (1995) *Designing Organizations: An executive briefing on strategy, structure, and process*, Jossey-Bass, San Francisco

Galbraith, J R (2000) *Designing the Global Organization*, Wiley, New York

Galbraith, J R (2010) The multi-dimensional and reconfigurable organization, *Organizational Dynamics*, 1 (2), 115–25

Kates, A and Galbraith, J R (2007) *Designing Your Organization: Using the Star Model to solve five critical design challenges*, Jossey-Bass, San Francisco

Kesler, G and Kates, A (2011) *Leading Organization Design: How to make organization design decisions to drive the results you want*, Jossey-Bass, San Francisco

Kesler, G and Kates, A (2016) *Bridging Organization Design and Performance: Five ways to activate a global operating model*, John Wiley & Sons, Inc, New York

Lawrence, P R and Lorsch, J W (1967) Differentiation and integration in complex organizations, *Administrative Science Quarterly*, 12 (1), 1–47

Ohnesorge, L (2019) It's done! IBM buys Red Hat; Whitehurst says "Red Hat is still Red Hat," Triangle Business Journal, July 9. www.bizjournals.com/triangle/news/2019/07/09/its-done-ibm-buys-red-hat-whitehurst-says-red-hat.html (archived at https://perma.cc/NXE4-349C)

Rigby, D, Elk, S, and Berez, S (2020) The agile c-suite: A new approach to leadership for the team at the top, *Harvard Business Review*, May–June

Stoll, J D (2019) For CEOS, it's a whole new job, *Wall Street Journal*, December 16. www.wsj.com/articles/the-new-difficult-role-of-the-ceo-11576516185 (archived at https://perma.cc/64C2-D42V)

Sull, D (2009) How to thrive in turbulent markets, *Harvard Business Review*, February

The Conference Board (2020) Survey: Business leaders start 2020 with lingering concerns about talent shortages and recession risk. www.conference-board.org/topics/c-suite-challenge/press/c-suite-survey-2020 (archived at https://perma.cc/KYV8-WZSV)

Operating Models

02

Transformation in strategy and organization was top of mind for many business leaders in the 2010s. The Coronavirus pandemic is accelerating many trends that were underway. While we certainly cannot make predictions, from our vantage point we expect to see more:

Innovative business models: Adoption of more consumer-oriented, digitally enabled channels, greater vertical integration, and more convergence of industries (e.g., media content *and* distribution).

Increased focus on integrated customer solutions: Bundling together product, services, and software into integrated solutions, with design-thinking incorporated into the user experience.

Digital learning and artificial intelligence: Incorporating digital and artificial intelligence deeply within the enterprise infrastructure, strengthening the entire value stream from strategy to product development, marketing and selling, and production and supply chain operations.

Ecosystem engagement: Extending the depth and breadth of the offering to include external partners in development and distribution of products and services that extend across boundaries, often with both cooperation and competition among the partners.

These forces lead to more complex business strategies, which in turn require more complex organizational arrangements. This is where ambition and execution often collide. Brilliant strategies that are not supported by well-designed and managed organizations soon burn out. Whether enabling a proactive strategic change or responding to an external threat, the leadership teams we see succeeding understand that they have to engage in the design and activation of the organization as vigorously as they engage in strategy and priority work. Design is about understanding the adjustments that need to be made around the Star Model to create a system to drive behavior and results. Activation is the on-going set of tactics that bring the organization design vision to life. Design and activation are an iterative process that ensures the organization is adaptive and dynamic (Kesler and Kates, 2016).

Design and activation start with a clear operating model that enables leadership to lay out an overall architecture of the relationship among the business components. In this chapter we will define an operating model and the design decisions and tools that allow leaders to develop well-considered and dynamic architecture for the organization.

The Operating Model

The operating model of a company is the basic organizational architecture that makes it possible to execute strategy at the enterprise, business-unit, and functional levels (Kesler and Kates, 2016). The operating model answers these questions:

1 What relationship of the business portfolio will deliver the most value to customers?

2 What capabilities are owned at the enterprise level, creating integration across the businesses, and which are owned at the business unit level?

3 What is the basic shape of the organization model?

4 Where should accountability for business results be placed in the organization?

5 What are the roles of business units, functions (operating and enabling), and markets?

6 What is the right balance of power across those components?

7 Where do we need integration and where do we want separation across lines of business?

8 What is the ecosystem within which this business operates, and what connections need to be made?

The operating model describes the relationship of the components of the company to one another, including relationships with customers, partners, competitors, and suppliers that extend beyond the walls of the corporation, as show in Figure 2.1.

Figure 2.1 The operating model

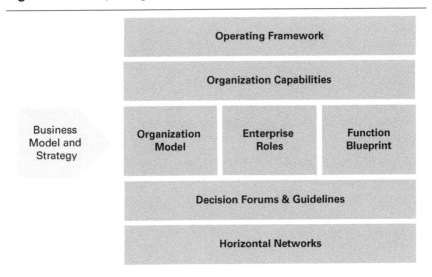

Perhaps the best way to articulate the importance of an operating model is to look at what happens when one is not defined. On several occasions, we have watched as large, successful but mature companies conduct exhaustive studies into existing cost structures, capital allocations, and asset footprints. The usual goal is to identify areas for efficiency gains and to refocus capital toward future growth priorities. Massive amounts of data are analyzed, and reports are returned to the executives, often with specific cost-reduction targets within the existing organizational structures. Operations managers, staff groups, and line leaders are handed extensive analysis with external benchmarks and improvement targets. In many cases, there is a transformation office that coordinates the campaign and assures that "value capture" is managed across the company toward the total objective.

Then, each set of leaders will often work within their silos to come up with initiatives to reach the goal. The leaders will meet together periodically to check progress, and in some cases they will collaborate across the silos to ensure that changes that affect their area are acceptable. The consolidation of procurement or outbound logistics are often areas of common interest.

But this process doesn't surface real tensions or put fundamental, hard decisions on the table. Proposed cost reductions in one part of the organization may come at the expense of another. Big opportunities across boundaries are often missed. For example, investing in a global product platform is unlikely to show up on anyone's cost reduction list. As the piece parts of the company incrementally reset the cost structure, it becomes harder and harder to accumulate enough initiatives to reach the ambitious benchmark targets.

We had the opportunity recently in a large industrial company to help leadership think through the company operating model in parallel to an exhaustive structural cost study. Our organizational findings and recommendations happened to be reviewed by the CEO and his executive committee in the afternoon of the same day they had reviewed the final cost targets (provided by another consultancy) in the morning. Our operating framework insights included the need to rethink the basic structure of the company's businesses and its global functions. At a very high level, the recommendations were roughly as follows:

- Shift from geography-centric profit and loss centers (P&Ls) to global product lines.

- Move to a more integrated organization with a shared commercial front-end and a shared operational back end in two of the four product divisions.

- Refocus the regional commercial organizations to be a sales and service organization.

- Establish center-led leadership across the regional engineering centers to drive platform development.

- Strengthen operations to manage a single production footprint, aligned around evolving product platforms.

- Establish a robust portfolio review and management process for the executive committee to set capital investment priorities across the divisions, aligned with growth prospects of each.

The afternoon was a true discovery moment for the CEO and team. Most of the executives immediately began to see how this major shift in the overall model would represent the kind of breakthrough that would allow them to attack costs at the structural level, and at the same time help to focus investments around the real growth opportunities. The cost analysis, by contrast, had provided useful data but not insight into the system as a whole.

The operating model is a direction, a blueprint; it is not an organization chart. All of that happens later. Rethinking the operating model with the big-picture view is a powerful, often indispensable, way to approach many transformational events:

- scaling or entering into an initial public offering of a growth company
- merging two companies
- shifting to a more (or less) vertically integrated business model
- spinning off a business to become a publicly traded, stand-alone company
- launching a major new enterprise-focused initiative
- turning around a troubled business

In every case, it means taking a top-down view of what the company's architecture should be and designing the whole with a view toward the future.

Operating Framework

The operating framework is the first step in the discussion. It makes clear assumptions about the relationship of the parts of the company. We find the operating framework is the best way to get a set of leaders to articulate and align on assumptions about what pieces and processes to connect and where to allow more autonomy.

We can depict operating framework choices along a simple continuum as shown in Figure 2.2. The left column represents a single integrated business and the right column represents a holding company. Between the extremes are closely and loosely related portfolios.

These four archetypes define the level of integration needed across the portfolio, based upon the extent to which the business models underlying each component are similar or different. Business models reflect how the company profits from different types of customers. Starting with strategy—how we serve customers and how we generate revenue—ensures that the design thinking starts with the customer in mind.

Where an organization sits on this continuum will determine the answers to questions like these:

- How much authority will be delegated from the center to operating units?
- How independent should different operating units be from each other?
- How much lateral and vertical integration and coordination is needed to deliver the required results and capabilities?
- What role will support functions play and with how much power and influence?

Figure 2.2 Operating framework continuum

	1 Fully Integrated Single Business	**2** Closely Related Portfolio	**3** Loosely Related Portfolio	**4** Holding Co or Conglomerate
Strategy & Org Design	Single strategy guides all P&L units with minor variations.	Complementary business portfolio and core strategies with synergies.	Diverse, relatively autonomous businesses set strategies, with limited synergies across units.	Structuring cheap finance, buying and selling separate assets.
Governance	Strategy and execution oversight comes from organizational center. All process and practices are common. Single culture.	Business units drive strategy and varying degrees of execution, often with shared resources (in a matrix). Seeks benefits of scale in core technologies, product and commercial platforms, and/or back-end operations.	Business units drive nearly full execution of results with limited matrix. Cross-BU scale is limited (e.g. government relations, technology transfer, back-end shared services). Some effort to harmonize culture.	Focused on appointing leaders. Business units return financials to parent. No common processes. Multiple cultures.
Role of the Center	Drives functional policy, staffing and standards to build a consistent global function presence across the company. Functional costs managed centrally.	Orchestrates and owns a common strategic agenda and most processes. Collaborates closely with divisions to support execution. Manages company-wide talent process and shared services. Influences functional cost structure.	Builds skills, tools, and talent practices necessary to strengthen a few functional capabilities. Priorities are guided mostly in divisions. May be a few selective shared services. Costs managed primarily within the business units.	Limited company-wide policies and practices mostly focused on risk and fiduciary matters.
Company Examples	Apple Heineken Coca-Cola	Siemens Deere & Co Medtronic Microsoft P&G PepsiCo	Aditya Birla Group Unilever United Technologies	Berkshire Hathaway Virgin Group

Companies that operate at the extreme left of the continuum tend to have a single business model and a structure built around business functions. Functional leaders in marketing, sales, engineering, and operations work as a single team to run the business. Diversity in the business tends to be geographic, or perhaps in vertical markets, or channels. The business functions drive decisions, and the enabling functions drive a high degree of commonality in policy and practice across the geographies.

Companies that operate at the extreme right of the continuum are holding companies or conglomerates. They are simple organizations at the enterprise level, with a very small corporate center focused on high-level talent and financial decisions.

The most complex design questions arise in the closely and loosely related portfolios. In these cases, business leaders want to allow some degree of business unit and market autonomy while gaining the benefits of resource leverage that come with shared functions and processes. In columns 2 and 3 in the framework (Figure 2.2), business units are often aligned by product or service offering or by customer types.

In the closely related portfolio (column 2), the business units are not fully independent, and they do not contain all of the functions necessary to run the business. Often, they are primarily focused on managing the offering, marketing, and product creation. In the loosely related portfolio, business units tend to be more autonomous, with most or all functional resources embedded and largely controlled in the business unit. They may share elements of the sales process or operations, but they tend to be more empowered, profit-and-loss units.

When times are tough and companies are looking to cut costs, leaders tend to move left on the operating framework continuum in the quest for greater integration and leverage across the business units. When companies are seeking to drive growth, they tend to loosen the reins from headquarters and move to the right. This allows each business greater degrees of flexibility.

Unfortunately, business leaders often tend to swing the pendulum across the operating-model continuum, as a reflection of leadership style or a reaction to apparent performance gaps, rather than as a conscious strategic change. The over-correction is perceived by employees as an inevitable oscillation between centralized and decentralized philosophies as different leadership regimes come and go. This can create cynicism and inconsistencies in the model that lead to confusion and unhealthy tension.

Figure 2.3 shows an example of a house-of-brands financial services company that has plans to leverage product development, technology, and operations across business units. Interviews with the leadership team show agreement on the direction of change—to move towards a more integrated company—but also a fairly wide range of perspectives on what moving to the left on the continuum really means.

Using the operating framework is a powerful way to start the conversation on what to connect and the nature of the new power dynamics across products, markets, and functions. This "how we will run the company" alignment discussion is a critical first step in the design process. The scope of the operating framework shift depicted above is substantial, and most leadership teams are overwhelmed by the task and unclear on how to proceed. Their instinct is to start to talk about management team structures and people, but we know that is premature in the design process. The four archetypes in the operating model framework set out the basic roles that business units, geographic territories, and corporate functions play in the company, and they define basic power relationships among these units. That is the right conversation to have at this stage.

The decision on which of the four options fits the business should be based on a number of factors. There is usually a "best fit" that reflects several considerations, given the company's history and strategy. Some examples highlight different choices that a company may make.

PepsiCo manages an operating model with a regional center of gravity. Consumer tastes, which remain highly diverse across cultures and geographies, demand a very "local" approach to brands and product innovation. Most food companies utilize a similar model. At PepsiCo, the corporate culture is also very entrepreneurial, sometimes even internally competitive. Efforts to move to a more integrated operating model have succeeded mostly among corporate functions such as procurement, finance, and human resources. Its food and beverage categories operate in a much more decentralized manner for strategic, cultural, even philosophical reasons—that may or may not be explicit. As an enterprise, PepsiCo is in column 2, but leaning toward column 3, a loosely related portfolio.

P&G and Unilever compete in similar consumer categories and both are quite international. But P&G has, despite some adjustments back and forth, chosen to maintain a highly center-led, global approach to managing its

Figure 2.3 Shifts in the operating framework for a financial services company

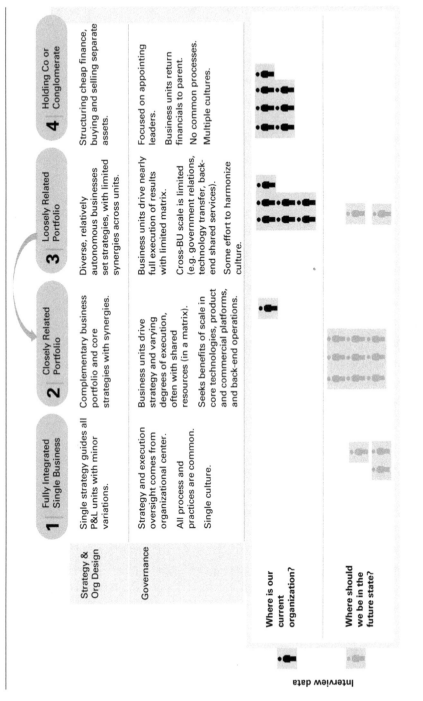

	1 Fully Integrated Single Business	**2** Closely Related Portfolio	**3** Loosely Related Portfolio	**4** Holding Co or Conglomerate
Strategy & Org Design	Single strategy guides all P&L units with minor variations.	Complementary business portfolio and core strategies with synergies.	Diverse, relatively autonomous businesses set strategies, with limited synergies across units.	Structuring cheap finance, buying and selling separate assets.
Governance	Strategy and execution oversight comes from organizational center. All process and practices are common. Single culture.	Business units drive strategy and varying degrees of execution, often with shared resources (in a matrix). Seeks benefits of scale in core technologies, product and commercial platforms, and back-end operations.	Business units drive nearly full execution of results with limited matrix. Cross-BU scale is limited (e.g. government relations, technology transfer, back-end shared services). Some effort to harmonize culture.	Focused on appointing leaders. Business units return financials to parent. No common processes. Multiple cultures.

Where is our current organization?

Where should we be in the future state?

Interview data

brands and innovation (column 2, closely related). P&G has largely exited the food business to focus on personal and homecare categories. Unilever, on the other hand, has intentionally maintained a much more regionally aligned operating model, reflecting a strong point of view that consumer differences across regions require a more regional approach to driving the same work (column 3, loosely related portfolio). It also has a more diverse set of products across food and consumer goods. So, the product portfolio, in itself, influences the choice, but it is not the only factor. Unilever's top leadership has for decades distrusted center-led governance, outside of a few core capabilities, and encourages leaders in its regions and country-based units to stay close to local tastes and choices in the way it adapts products and marketing messages. Increasingly, Unilever seeks efficiencies in its operations, and it does adhere to some core philosophies and practices, but category management remains a largely local affair.

3M is an example of a column 3, loosely related portfolio company with a diverse set of products and go-to-market channels sitting on a highly integrated technology platform, in this case chemical and materials technology. Advances in abrasives, adhesives, films, and fluoromaterial find their way into multiple products and applications, which serve both business-to-business customers and consumers. 3M recently announced additions to its so-called "periodic table of technology platforms," now boasting 51 elements. They reside in a single technology organization, aligned around materials, processing, digital, and applications capabilities. The product-aligned business units remain quite autonomous, but the technology organization is a binding force at 3M.

Apple, in contrast, operates in column 1, single business, in the operating model continuum. It runs a highly center-led operating model. Its products, services, and ecosystem are well served by this governing approach, despite the increasing diversity of its offerings. And it adheres to a strong center-led philosophy that has created perhaps the most valuable brand in the world.

The holding company, to the far-right side of the continuum, is a rapidly decreasing segment of American and European business. Most true holding companies are based in Asia today, and many are still family-held. In the US, investors have shunned conglomerates, and many have broken up or divested significant assets in recent years, notably General Electric, Honeywell, United Technologies, Dupont/Dow, Alcoa, and Danaher. Investors have rewarded focus. Investors want the predictability of share performance that a focused portfolio provides. As a result, an interesting trend we have noticed is that even holding companies are seeking ways to integrate in order to leverage scale. Berkshire Hathaway, famous for the independence of the business units within the portfolio, has started to leverage assets. Top executives from the businesses meet to share strategies and best practices on topics as diverse as purchasing, sustainability, cybersecurity, hiring practices, and healthcare costs (Friedman, 2019).

Amazon, Alibaba, Alphabet, and other tech giants have forged a different path for the holding company, using platforms to link together a highly diversified business portfolio. Consider Amazon's purchase of Whole Foods, which stands as a separate business unit from its core e-business organization, both of which are separate from Amazon Web Services and the Prime entertainment content business. But, these and other offerings as diverse as Zappos and Audible all sit on a shared customer-data platform and digital and AI backbone. Clearly, "competitive advantage is increasingly defined by the ability to shape and control digital networks" (Iansiti and Lakhani, 2020.) Companies that can connect businesses effectively are able to aggregate data that move among them, wresting value out of analytics and artificial intelligence. Alphabet, for all practical purposes, is a holding company today, and its venture businesses (autonomous vehicles, healthcare, fiber, etc.) operate independently from each other and the core Google products. But, be assured they are integrated through Google's Cloud business and their many network connections, gaining insight across diverse industries with a core of data and unified code.

United Technologies is another interesting conglomerate. It shifted its operating model in 2019–20 from an aggregation of aerospace, jet engines, elevators, and heating and air-conditioning brands, to a more focused aerospace company, accomplished through the spinoff of Otis and Carrier and the acquisition of Rockwell Collins aerospace. But before the new operating model could be activated, the opportunistic merger with Raytheon was structured, shifting the portfolio back to a more diverse collection of defense and commercial businesses featuring missiles and complex guidance and radar systems, along with jet engines and aerospace products and services. The new business strategy was built on finding substantial technology synergies.

The CEO of United Technologies, Greg Hayes (who became the CEO of the new Raytheon Technologies), consciously worked through a series of iterations to define the right operating model for each entity as the company re-invented itself twice in a 12-month period, through simultaneous divestitures and acquisitions. Hayes was determined to get it right, and while he remained consistent in his philosophical view that business units should be the strong center of gravity, and that support functions should be very lean at the corporate layer, he shifted gears and crafted a different, more decentral-ized operating model for the new and diverse aerospace and defense com-pany that would become Raytheon Technologies. A significant part of the business case in this acquisition was focused on technology transfer (not cost synergies) among jet propulsion, missiles, GPS, and radar systems. With the help of his chief human resources officer, Hayes had become a believer in defining a clear organizational architecture that would guide the right deci-sions about where to place portions of engineering, digital technology, as well as the support functions in the operating units and at the enterprise level. Acquisition integration teams would follow that playbook as they worked to merge the substantial infrastructure of the two companies.

Even some of the family conglomerates that use the portfolio approach to diversify their holdings are moving toward more integration. One that has been thoughtful and creative in this regard is Aditya Birla Group (ABG), based in Mumbai. ABG has 18 business units and 120,000 employees in 36 countries. Half of its $41 billion in revenue comes from outside India. Businesses range from metals, mining, cement, and chemicals to financial services, telecom, fashion, and retail. On the surface it looks like a classic holding company.

ABG leaders are well aware of the dangers that have tripped up other conglomerates that dared to chase synergies: a bloated corporate center, slow decisions, sub-optimized performance, lots of one-size-fits-none solu-tions, and wasted energy arguing about corporate controls and onerous al-locations. Yet, they see opportunities to leverage the scale and scope of these diverse assets for the new, digitally enabled economy that will be the future of India. Some of these are customer linkages. For example, how can they take their 400 million telecom customers and connect them to their financial services and retail businesses? Some of the linkages are rooted in technology. How can they leverage innovations they are developing in chemicals into the cement business and create new sustainable and energy efficient building materials?

ABG is using its corporate functions to be the conduits of talent and ideas for innovation. Each function is designed with a different, yet purposeful, relationship to the business units and countries. Here are a just a few exam-ples ranging from a light touch at the center to highly directive.

Data and analytics: For this new capability, the belief is that this work has to stay close to the business. The data and analytics corporate function has the remit to foster start-up projects and encourage the businesses to learn what they need. The plan is that as this capability matures, the center can plan a more direct role in leveraging expertise and guiding investments.

Procurement: Procurement across such a diversified portfolio doesn't lend itself to centralization and ABG leadership is careful not to push common processes where they don't add value. A community of practice among procurement leaders is a light-touch mechanism to build professional identity and connections and allow coordinated buying to be undertaken where it makes sense.

IT: IT is also largely embedded in the business units. Corporate IT largely serves as the interface to the larger ecosystem for cloud and shared systems. Although digital and other new technologies are important to all ABG businesses, leadership is careful not to give too much power to the center. Corporate IT has to constantly demonstrate value and prove why a service it offers isn't better housed in a business unit or provided by a vendor.

Innovation center: A corporate innovation center functions as a true center of expertise. Businesses units tap into best practices in new product development and the center actively facilitates connections and conversations across boundaries.

Human resources: HR is completely centralized. It is charged with developing executive talent, moving talent, and building attractive careers. The "Chairman's Series" is a sophisticated leadership academy focused on building global mindsets, digital expertise, and organization design skills along with strategy and finance depth. The 300 top leaders come together frequently in these forums to learn, build networks, and share ideas.

Building Out the Operating Model

Aligning on the relationship of the parts of the business portfolio and where integration and separation will create value for customers is a start. But the operating framework is not nearly granular enough to fully define a new organizational architecture. An executive team then needs to work through a set of tools that force the right conversations to answer the questions we posed earlier (Figure 2.4).

To be clear, this is an iterative process. It rarely unfolds in a tidy, linear fashion. One component is defined and then another; the team may go back and rework prior drafts as the overall shape of the new organization be-

Figure 2.4 The operating model and the questions it answers

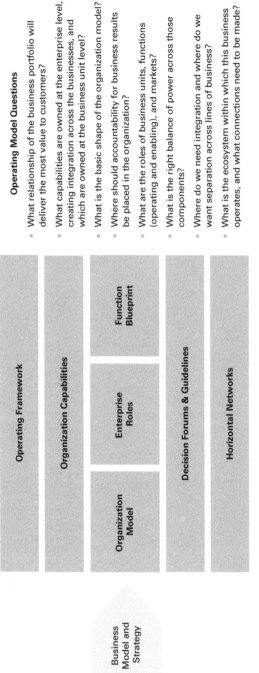

Operating Model Questions

- What relationship of the business portfolio will deliver the most value to customers?

- What capabilities are owned at the enterprise level, creating integration across the businesses, and which are owned at the business unit level?

- What is the basic shape of the organization model?

- Where should accountability for business results be placed in the organization?

- What are the roles of business units, functions (operating and enabling), and markets?

- What is the right balance of power across those components?

- Where do we need integration and where do we want separation across lines of business?

- What is the ecosystem within which this business operates, and what connections need to be made?

Operating Framework

Organization Capabilities

Function Blueprint

Enterprise Roles

Organization Model

Decision Forums & Guidelines

Horizontal Networks

Business Model and Strategy

comes clearer. Ownership and commitment to the model are critical in completing this work. The CEO or leader of the business unit being designed must be engaged; he or she will take positions on key questions and at the same time allow others to put their fingerprints on the drafts as they evolve. Let's introduce the rest of the components of the operating model, which will each be further explored in subsequent chapters.

Enterprise Organizational Capabilities

Capabilities have long been the focus of organization designers seeking to anchor structure, process, rewards, and people to a strategy (Kates and Galbraith, 2007). Capabilities are the organizational muscles needed to execute strategy. Companies such as P&G have made capabilities an explicit part of their corporate strategy, a kind of competitive DNA.

Capabilities are more likely to be owned and managed at the enterprise level in the closely related portfolio in the operating framework because they can be shared across businesses. In more loosely coupled portfolios, competitive capabilities are more likely to be owned by individual business units. However, as we have discussed earlier, even the holding company may focus on a handful of enabling capabilities, such as risk management, efficient capital allocation, or talent management.

In VF Corp, CEO Steve Rendle identified what he called "mega-choices," a set of enterprise capabilities including retail excellence, supply chain agility, brand experience, and design innovation. VF is a house of global apparel brands, including North Face, Vans, and Timberland, each managed as a business. But these enterprise capabilities apply to all of the brands and can be built once for the entire portfolio. Rendle assigned an executive committee member to be a sponsor for each of these capabilities, forcing a degree of interdependence across the business units. VF Corp is a closely related portfolio of brands. Empowered, global brand business units are the center of gravity providing local agility. But the leveraged, shared capabilities that serve all categories and brands provide scale. Chapter 9 provides examples of how to build new enterprise capabilities.

Organization Model

An organization model is an illustration of the central design concept. The simple idea is to identify the major components of the organization and the nature of the power relationships among them. The organization model provides a high-level answer to the following questions:

- What units own the product and/or service offering, and how are they aligned?
- What units own the customer and the go-to-market process?
- What units own fulfillment and technology?
- What are the enabling functions that support the business?

We explore organization models in Chapter 3, with a focus on the front/back model, a useful starting point for complex organizations (Figure 2.5).

Enterprise Roles

The work of the company's major organizational units (business units, regions/channels, and functions) can and should be outlined at a high level—on a single page, so that one can easily read across those roles to understand what each will do, relative to the other. We like the format in Figure 2.6, but there are other ways to lay it out. The roles need to be specific enough that the picture is clear but lean enough that executives will actually read it and take their "red pencils" to it in order to make it their own. This work is a natural part of the organization model discussion and further discussed in Chapter 3.

Function Blueprint

After the model takes shape around the core business roles, it makes sense to think about the major support functions. The leadership team of each function will eventually need to complete deep design work to create a service delivery model that fits the needs of the enterprise and the operating units. But these teams should not work completely independently of each other. Rather, they should start with an overall blueprint that lays out a common design logic. One key design consideration is where functional work is to be placed. What will sit in the business units (for agility), what will be consolidated (for scale), and where will we embed lean functional, digitally enabled infrastructure in order to avoid unnecessary layering? Figure 2.7 shows an example of a tool that is often helpful in this regard.

Figure 2.5 The front/back model

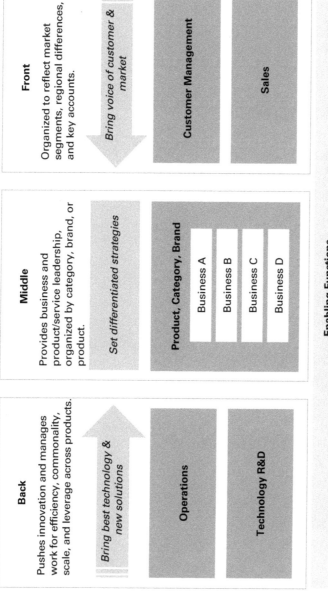

Back

Pushes innovation and manages work for efficiency, commonality, scale, and leverage across products.

Bring best technology & new solutions

Operations

Technology R&D

Middle

Provides business and product/service leadership, organized by category, brand, or product.

Set differentiated strategies

Product, Category, Brand

Business A

Business B

Business C

Business D

Front

Organized to reflect market segments, regional differences, and key accounts.

Bring voice of customer & market

Customer Management

Sales

Enabling Functions
(HR, Finance, IT, Legal, Communications, etc.)

Figure 2.6 Enterprise role definition example

	Enterprise Leadership (Executive Team)	Product Divisions	Region/Markets	Enabling Functions
Strategy	Sets the growth strategy. Allocates capital to increase long-term shareholder value. Sets culture and values for the company.	Anchor business unit layer owning product/service offering. Develops and deploys global growth and profit strategies within the business unit. Drives aligned product and service platform innovation strategies and plans.	Sets commercial strategy for assigned geography. Owns in-market customer relationships.	Creates functional strategies to build critical capabilities and deliver scaled services and automation. Ensures compliance to protect enterprise interests.
Execution	Sets growth, margin, and cash objectives by division and region, aligned with shareholder commitments.	Manages product development programs. Works with regions to set growth and profit targets for offerings. Supports execution with regions and owns the product profitability through the life cycle.	Sets growth plans for the geography. Executes local strategies consistent with global strategies. Bundles solutions to meet local customer needs, consistent with global standards. Owns regional results.	Enables success of business objectives with effective decision support. Drives consistent processes and captures scale benefits with shared services and expertise. Manages central operational functions.
Decision Authority	Sets growth and productivity investment priorities and targets. Defines the operating model for the company.	Sets product road map. Sets pricing guidelines. Sets global service standards. Collaborates with functions and regions to set growth/profit targets for products.	Defines replicable product and service solutions that meet customer needs profitably. Works with product divisions to set annual targets.	Sets functional standards and ways of working. Makes functional appointments to key roles. Sets a cost envelope for the function worldwide.
Talent	Oversees key talent pools and succession across the enterprise. Owns key leader selection and development.	Manages talent in the interest of the business unit and builds marketing/product management skill sets.	Oversees talent movement and development within a region, supporting enterprise talent objectives.	Ensures cross-regional view of talent development. Owns function succession plans for the company, working with products and regions.

Figure 2.7 Functional blueprint example

Level	HR	Finance	IT	Legal
Corporate Layer *Focus: policy, compliance, critical centers of expertise, and selected shared services.*	Policy & Compliance Corporate COEs HR Ops	Policy & Compliance FP&A Resources Treasury, Tax, Audit, etc.	Architecture, Policy/Compliance Enterprise Functionality IT Support Services	Policy & Compliance Partner Mgt. Advisory
Division Layer *Span-breaking, supervisory layer.*	HR Business Partner	Fin. Business Partner	BU Specific Applications	Region Counsel
Region or BU *Span-breaking, supervisory layer.*		Shared Services and COEs		
Country *Focus: meeting local needs efficiently.*	HR Business Partner	Fin. Business Partner	IT Business Partner	

The functions take their lead in doing this work from the operating framework, organization model, and enterprise roles work already completed. If we are building an operating model that fits column 2 in the operating framework, the "closely related portfolio," then the functional architecture will lean toward more center-led functions and likely more shared centers of expertise and service. Business units will be skinny, with few fully controlled, embedded functional players. If, on the other hand, we are building a column 3, "loosely related portfolio" model, then each business unit is likely to have more dedicated functional resources. This guidance should be evident in the functional blueprint.

Once the blueprint is established, with a top-down view, then the separate functions can go to work in a bottom-up deep dive into their processes, staffing levels, and technology to redesign themselves in a consistent manner, utilizing a single vision. This topic is discussed in more depth in Chapter 6.

Decision Forums and Guidelines

The objective of this part of the operating model is three-fold:

1 Clearly differentiate the value that the senior leadership layers bring to the company, in order to avoid overlaps and unnecessary complexity that are likely to inhibit speed.

2 Identify the anchor layer in the operating model; this is the layer of general management that is fully accountable for business results (Kesler and Kates, 2016). It is often the strategic business unit, where cross-functional business management is necessary, and it should not be confused with aggregated or span-breaking groups of businesses.

3 Define the decision-making, operational, and innovation forums that will be key parts of the operating model.

We start the design of decision forums by defining the work of leadership. A simple view of the unique contribution of each layer, as shown in Figure 2.8, creates a frame to force choices about the work of layer. For example, the integrative layer should be very enterprise focused. In a large, complex, and matrixed company, the leaders in the integrative layer oversee enterprise talent and other critical processes that tie the units together. They may manage large enterprise-level innovation and other initiatives. CEOs who call out an integrative layer often include an extended executive leadership team that reaches below the CEO's direct reports in order to create more direct connections between the businesses and the top of the house. This critical mass of senior leaders can be a very powerful means of driving change or executing a new growth strategy.

Figure 2.8 Unique contributions of each layer of leadership

Strategic Leadership Layer

- Set the vision, manage the portfolio, set clear direction, priorities, and culture
- Make big bet and trade-off decisions
- Communicate purpose with one voice.

 Time horizon: 5–10 Years

Integrative Leadership Layer

- Manage the forums, systems, processes, and ways of working to drive horizontal, structured collaboration across boundaries.

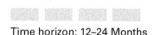 Time horizon: 2–5 Years

Anchor Business Layer (Operating Layer)

- Serve customers profitably
- Enable teams with direction, resources, coaching, and clarity—consistent with enterprise guidance.

Time horizon: 12–24 Months

The design of the vertical structure and how this enables empowerment and speed in decision-making is covered in Chapter 4.

Horizontal Networks

The final piece to the operating model is the design of the various planning, decision-making, and review forums. Designing these conversations and the structured networks across organization and geographic boundaries is hard, but critical, work. It is rarely a once-and-done process. Rather, connecting the organization horizontally for high-value collaboration requires good design, but it also requires courageous leaders that set out behavioral expectations, model them, and hold others accountable. Building horizontal networks requires reflection and learning, and an investment in trust.

Unfortunately, while many leaders want to see more collaboration in their organizations, they allow their teams to get caught up in simplistic debates over whether to centralize or decentralize. The reality is that today's organizations must deliver the benefits of both. One of the best ways to do this is to add "center-led" to the design vocabulary, as shown in Figure 2.9.

Figure 2.9 Center-led distinguishes integration from control

	Low	Control	High
Global (Integration)	**Center-Led** Single strategy, common process and tools, clear decision guard rails, empowered teams (freedom within a framework).		Centralized Policy, fiduciary controls, centralized reporting.
Local (Integration)	De-Centralized Autonomous business units with little functional or central guidance and little synergy expected.		High Control, Low Integration Bureaucracy.

Of course, centralization of work and decisions (high control with high integration) is sometimes appropriate. When ensuring an enterprise perspective and common standards, this centralization is critical. Risk management, ethics, and brand boundaries are all examples of work that is often centralized. Decentralizing work and decisions (low control and integration) is appropriate when the center (headquarters or corporate) can add little or no value to the work of the operating unit or where common ways of working don't provide value to the customer.

Companies in the lower-right quadrant of the model exhibit high degrees of control with low levels of integration. Working across boundaries to serve customers, to innovate with bigger ideas, and to drive brand value is very difficult. Employees and managers in these companies often report in organization assessments that they are constrained by controls that cause the organization to labor too hard on simple things that add no value to the customers. In other words, these organizations suffer the worst of both worlds: low degrees of collaboration with slow, overly controlled decision-making.

Enter the center-led concept. In the center-led approach, there are high degrees of collaboration across business and functional units, enabled by shared strategy, a common agenda, harmonized processes, and a close-knit culture. When work and decisions are center-led, those with enterprise roles support the operating units to coordinate and collaborate. They provide the forums, the data, and the tools to make good trade-offs that serve customers profitably.

While these center-led roles have appropriate controls and compliance mechanisms at their disposal, they do not over-rely on them. When done well, this construct can be very empowering for the operating units, an outcome characterized as "freedom in a framework." Teams are enabled by the center to make good decisions fast for the customer, with a minimum of administrative oversight.

The design of horizontal networks is new for many leaders. Therefore, we devote one-third of the book to this topic. Chapter 5 (The Horizontal Organization), Chapter 7 (Metrics), and Chapter 8 (Leadership and culture) go deeply into how to design for collaborative behaviors.

Key Takeaways

- The operating model provides the overall architecture for how the business will be run.

- The operating framework makes clear how closely the components of the business portfolio need to be connected.

- Enterprise capabilities are the new muscles that will drive execution of the business strategy.

- The organization model depicts the major groupings of work and how they are intended to relate to customers, competitors, and technologies.

- Enterprise roles lay out accountabilities for major units.

- The function blueprint depicts where infrastructure will be in the layers of the organization.

- Decision forums and guidelines create the balance of boundaries and empowerment for good, fast decisions and make clear the role of each organization layer in decision-making.

- Horizontal networks are the structured connections, enabled from the center, that move ideas, knowledge, and talent across organization boundaries and geographic borders.

References

Friedman, N (2019) The Berkshire empire is quietly collaborating more than ever, *Wall Street Journal*, 4 April. www.wsj.com/articles/the-berkshire-empire-is-quietly-collaborating-more-than-ever-11554370201 (archived at https://perma.cc/37UC-Y2HT)

Iansiti, M and Lakhani, K R (2020) Competing in the age of AI, *Harvard Business Review*, January–February. https://hbr.org/2020/01/competing-in-the-age-of-ai (archived at https://perma.cc/NY5B-8AKA)

Kates, A and Galbraith, J R (2007) *Designing Your Organization: Using the Star Model to solve 5 critical design challenges*, Jossey-Bass, San Francisco

Kesler, G and Kates, A (2016) *Bridging Organization Design and Performance: Five ways to activate a global operating model*, John Wiley & Sons, Inc, New York

Organization Models

03

Organizations are invisible, abstract constructs. An organization is not the tangible product it produces, the services it delivers, or the physical locations in which it is housed. An organization is not even the people that identify with it. The people can change, but the organization is still there.

The organization exists because we believe it does. Yuval Harari (2015) says that what distinguishes humans from other animals is our ability to have "shared imagination." Shared imagination is what allows us to believe in invisible constructs such as money, religion, and nations. And, just like these other ideas, the organization exists solely because we accept as true that it does.

As organization designers, we face the challenge of making this invisible and abstract idea tangible enough for a group of leaders to imagine the nature of the future organization they are trying to create together. Words are important but often imprecise. Ask any random set of managers to define terms such as "matrix," "shared services," "network," "business unit," "agile," or even "team" and you are likely to get a variety of definitions and emotional responses depending upon each person's past experience with these concepts. Graphics help, but they are also only inadequate representations.

Even though it is difficult, rendering the organization is still a valuable exercise. We find that using a combination of both words and pictures early in the design process can help a design team explore and articulate organizational ideas. It is the very act of struggling to explain and build on ideas together that is useful. And then, long after the ideas have been turned into organization charts and job descriptions, these early expressions of intent often remain some of the best ways to communicate the core concepts of the new organization.

We call these conceptual combinations of words and pictures an "organization model." The organization model is a visual manifestation of how the parts of the organization are intended to relate. It is both a design tool and a communication tool. Building an organization model together allows leaders to work through new accountabilities and interdependencies without talking about specific jobs and people. It is true design work, bringing together the creative and analytical sides of the brain and benefiting from many diverse perspectives.

One of the biggest mistakes that leaders make in the organization design process is to start with their direct report structure and then assign work units to them based on the perceived strengths of the people on the leadership team. This is classic "designing around people" and yields designs that lack logic and have to be redone when there is a change of people at the top. Certainly, the organization chart is an important output of the design process. But it is not a design tool in the way that an organization model is.

In this chapter we will cover:

- what is an organization model, why it is important, and how it fits into the design process
- the front/back model and its variations

An Organization Model Example

Development of the organization model typically comes after creation or refinement of the strategy, identification of capabilities, and assessment of the current state. It is often developed iteratively with a discussion of the operating framework, discussed in Chapter 2. The act of creating the organization model can highlight where a leadership team is out of alignment regarding the relationship of the parts of the business portfolio. We have assumptions about the operating framework, we illustrate it through the organization model, and then we discover insights about our shared assumptions.

The group developing the organization model explores how different configurations and relationships between the parts of the organization will yield new behaviors, decisions, and business results. The organization models become a set of hypotheses that can be detailed and tested.

The W L Gore story will show how organization models are used in the design process. Gore is a privately held company founded in 1958, with nearly 10,000 associates operating in 40 countries and over $3 billion in sales. The company makes hundreds of components and products, all sharing a core technology based on polytetrafluoroethylene (PTFE). PTFE is a fluorine and carbon polymer that, when expanded, creates a microporous membrane with a high strength-to-weight ratio, compatibility with the human body, and excellent thermal and chemical resistance. (We have worked with Gore from 2016 to 2020. The information shared here is drawn from publicly available materials and a presentation in April 2018 at the Organization Design Forum conference by Gore leaders.)

The many products Gore sells, all based on this polymer, are grouped into three business units:

Medical: Implantable medical devices including stent grafts and vascular repair devices.

Fabrics: Sophisticated materials, from the flagship Gore-Tex brand to fabrics used by fire fighters, astronauts, and the military.

Performance solutions: Mostly industrial products such as filters, sealants, and gaskets, but also specialty products from guitar strings to dental floss.

Gore is a product innovation company, but is equally known for its highly evolved culture. Founder Bill Gore instilled some principles and unique practices that remain in place today. These include:

- No titles. Everyone at Gore is an "associate." Some associates are leaders. That's it.

- No job descriptions. Each associate makes their own commitments. For a long time, these were self-defined. Associates would find the projects they wanted to work on in their area and put together their personal portfolio of work. Today, there are job categories and work is more directed by leaders, but associates still have a significant say in what they work on.

- Peer review. Performance is assessed through 360-degree feedback. While a complex and lengthy process, it is a deep part of the culture that underscores the value that the company puts on collaboration.

- Lattice. Rather than organization charts and reporting lines, Gore has used the concept of a lattice of communications, in which people are connected in many more ways than typically seen in other organizations. As part of the lattice, everyone has a sponsor focused on their career development.

- Power of small teams. Bill Gore believed strongly that work is best done in small, highly autonomous teams. Even the size of manufacturing plants was limited to 150 people, based on Dunbar's law of relationships.

As a result, Gore remains one of the most organically collaborative organizations that we have ever worked with. Long before the technology companies of the 2000s made Agile teams all the rage, Gore was truly agile. Gore is a company in which one person with a compelling idea can attract others and form a team. These small, cross-disciplinary teams created and brought products to market.

In 2015, however, a number of factors prompted senior leaders to look at the organization, and the culture they had created. They found that:

- Productivity didn't match revenue growth. Assets weren't leveraged. Improvement activities yielded one-off solutions. Strong values created a strong sense of identity, but also a wide variety in ways of work and business processes. This inconsistency between business units and teams created cost.

- The bottom-up strategy yielded many small wins, but markets demanded bigger bets and clearer strategy. The medical device business unit was in a highly regulated environment and competed against the might of Medtronic and its enormous R&D budget. The fabrics industry was becoming a low margin business in a time of fast fashion and a broadening definition of "performance" in the marketplace. Gore-Tex was losing its cache as a brand. By being confined to the very high end of the market, growth was limited. And the performance solutions business was a hodgepodge of products, with a few big winners, but also many legacy projects started with good intent that had been left to linger without strict portfolio management.

- The culture of autonomy and independent small teams was actually causing frustration among associates. When Gore was small and led by a strong founder, autonomy was balanced by guidance from the top. New leaders, though able and respected, didn't have the mechanisms in place to substitute for the founder's vision. As the company grew in size, and product and customer complexity, the lack of common direction and coordination between teams made it harder to get work done overall.

Terri Kelly, the CEO at the time, made clear that the company's relatively small size and competitive global environment required it to act like more of a closely related portfolio rather than the loosely related portfolio that had characterized the company through much of its history. This declaration of a change in operating framework was a significant decision. She communicated clearly the belief that the company would keep its strong cultural tenets and business unit focus, but it would also find ways to leverage assets

Figure 3.1 Operating framework showing Gore's 2015 shift

	1 | Fully Integrated Single Business	2 | Closely Related Portfolio	3 | Loosely Related Portfolio	4 | Holding Co or Conglomerate
Strategy & Org Design	Single strategy guides all P&L units with minor variations.	Complementary business portfolio and core strategies with synergies.	Diverse, relatively autonomous businesses set strategies, with limited synergies across units.	Structuring cheap finance, buying and selling separate assets.
Governance	Strategy and execution oversight comes from organizational center. All process and practices are common. Single culture.	Business units drive strategy and varying degrees of execution, often with shared resources (in a matrix). Seeks benefits of scale in core technologies, product and commercial platforms, and/or back-end operations.	Business units drive nearly full execution of results with limited matrix. Cross-BU scale is limited (e.g. government relations, technology transfer, back-end shared services). Some effort to harmonize culture.	Focused on appointing leaders. Business units return financials to parent. No common processes. Multiple cultures.
Role of the Center	Drives functional policy, staffing and standards to build a consistent global function presence across the company. Functional costs managed centrally.	Orchestrates and owns a common strategic agenda and most processes. Collaborates closely with divisions to support execution. Manages company-wide talent process and shared services. Influences functional cost structure.	Builds skills, tools, and talent practices necessary to strengthen a few functional capabilities. Priorities are guided mostly in divisions. May be a few selective shared services. Costs managed primarily within the business units.	Limited company-wide policies and practices mostly focused on risk and fiduciary matters.
Company Examples	Apple Heineken Coca-Cola	Siemens Microsoft Deere & Co P&G Medtronic PepsiCo	Aditya Birla Group Unilever United Technologies	Berkshire Hathaway Virgin Group

and talent across the business portfolio. Leaders, working together, would provide stronger direction on what work would be pursued and how teams would be staffed. The company would still look like a loosely held portfolio given the diversity of its businesses, but leadership would work together as in a closely related portfolio, as shown in Figure 3.1.

Productivity and innovation are compelling reasons to work together, but integration is expensive. It requires more management time for planning and coordination. A move to the left on the continuum has to be quickly followed by an honest discussion of what parts of the organization need to be linked and which will remain more autonomous.

The organization model is the best way to have and illustrate this discussion. Gore leaders made three key decisions with respect to how the organization model would reflect the realities of their diverse business dynamics while simultaneously driving behaviors associated with a closely related business portfolio:

- The three businesses would remain as distinct units. This was important as each has a unique set of customers, competitors, and go-to-market practices. For example, medical devices require intricate piece-parts manufacturing, in a highly regulated industry where products are produced in expensive "clean rooms." Fabrics is a high-volume, bulk processing, low-margin business, where manufacturing costs needs to be kept down. Therefore, business strategy, product development, manufacturing, sales, and marketing remained in the business units.

- Three business functions—manufacturing, research and development (R&D), and sales and marketing—would have, for the first time, enterprise leadership focused on leveraging common assets, functional excellence, and talent development. New roles were created to oversee the creation of common ways of work and to build talent networks across the business units. For example, the sales and marketing leader was to direct the implementation of Salesforce and sales excellence training. The process of setting targets and directing deals would remain in the business units, however.

- Finally, the enabling functions, including human resources (HR), information technology (IT), legal, and safety, were to be managed completely at an enterprise level. The intention was to reduce costly variations in local practices that were no longer adding value to the whole company. While the consolidation of enabling functions is a difficult task in any company, it was particularly controversial at Gore, where associates were used to local, high-touch support.

Figure 3.2 Gore enterprise organization model

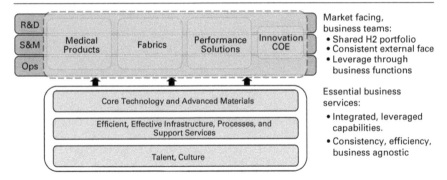

Market facing, business teams:
• Shared H2 portfolio
• Consistent external face
• Leverage through business functions

Essential business services:
• Integrated, leveraged capabilities.
• Consistency, efficiency, business agnostic

Figure 3.2 depicts these new relationships and design concepts for Gore at the enterprise level.

One of the most important uses of the organization model is to show power relationships and points of integration. In the Gore model, accountability for the profit and loss (P&L) sits squarely with the business units. But some power was moved out of the business units in order to change how decisions are made. The new business and enabling function leader roles were to have authority over investments in common systems, platforms, and processes intended to increase productivity and focus energy on bigger innovations and changes.

The business functions are shown as horizontals woven into the business units. The enabling functions and core technology, where the PTFE is produced, are foundational horizontals. This was intentionally done to indicate two different types of integration.

The business functions are highly connected to the business units. For example, manufacturing is run by each business unit. Questions now can be asked around power dynamics, such as: What is the scope of authority and work of the enterprise manufacturing leader and team? How will a network of manufacturing expertise be formed across business units? What decisions will this network take part in? How will we measure the success of the manufacturing horizontal?

The enabling functions are more separate from the business units. This leads to a different set of integration questions, such as: How will we set priorities for IT work across the business units? How will the voice of the business units be represented in enterprise decisions? What is the process for determining which practices are best practices and become enterprise ways of work?

All of these questions get answered as we design the details of the organization. It is the creation of the organization model, however, that allows us to even conceive of and ask the right questions. We will come back to Gore after we step back and consider the basic and emerging building blocks of structure and what we call the front/back organization model.

The Building Blocks of Complex Organizations

Organization models are created from a set of structural building blocks. The four basic types of structures are:

- Function: Work grouped by related activity or expertise. Functional groups allow for specialization, clear career paths, and strong professional identity.

- Geography: Work managed with a territorial boundary, which could be site, region, country, cluster, or continent. Geographical grouping makes the most sense when the product has to be highly localized in terms of features or go-to-market practices.

- Product: Product/service lines are multi-functional teams with accountability for developing products that can win in a specific market. Managing work by product often yields a strong focus on innovation and competitors.

- Customer: Customer groupings may reflect users, consumer segments, or industry verticals. The customer structure is a multi-function team focused on understanding and meeting unique customer needs.

More depth and detail regarding the basic structure building blocks and how each shapes organization behavior can be found in the book *Leading Organization Design* (Kesler and Kates, 2011).

These structures still cover most work, but we are observing some changes that are adding new vocabulary around digital, platforms and ecosystems, solutions, and channels.

The first is "digital." Digital is not a function. It isn't IT. It is a set of systems and new ways of working and interacting with customers enabled by new tools. We are in a transition time. In the future, we will likely stop talking about digital because it will no longer be something new or a place we aspire to go. Digital will be woven into the fabric of nearly all businesses.

But, because becoming "digital" for most companies is still a significant, multi-year journey, it requires leadership and focus. What makes digital important from an organization perspective is that it lives in various parts of the company that today are usually owned by multiple functional leaders. Digital lives in marketing through customer and consumer engagement and data analytics, in manufacturing through automation and robotics, in product development in the form of sensors and internet of things, and in sales through machine learning-guided customer service. In the enabling functions, digital is changing the core processes of the way work is done and how the company interacts with employees.

As a result, digital is causing a blurring of lines between functions and creating new functions. When 80 percent of technology spending is outside of the control of the IT function, and we expect that most employees will soon be working alongside technology inside and outside the company, then all strategy essentially becomes technology strategy. For example, traditionally, the folks in core IT infrastructure and those in marketing didn't need to work together very much. IT provided the connectivity for desktop applications or perhaps a customer relationship management system. Today, however, marketing is technology. Few marketing departments still have a separate digital group—it is all digital. New points of tension are created as a result. Who has authority over the many vendors, agencies, and partners that today's marketing department has to be connected with? Where do the people who program and customize systems and applications live and who manages them?

The other development in the past few years that has introduced new terminology is the concept of multi-sided platforms, which facilitate interactions or transactions between parties. Amazon, Alibaba, and Airbnb are well-known platforms in which the core of the business is to connect consumers to external vendors. Cloud technology is allowing many traditional companies to add a platform element to their business, creating much more complex ecosystems with blurred boundaries between what is internal and what is external to the company.

Conversely, solutions are highly integrated sets of products and services that are brought together for a customer. While the components are typically created or sourced by product units, they are often assembled and delivered by customer units. Management of the offering becomes a new task sitting between product and customer.

Finally, for many businesses, channels have become more complex. Companies managing wholesale and retail, through partnerships, and direct-to-consumer find that meeting the customer "where they are" creates significant internal complexity.

In the future, there will be additional dimensions within organizations. But the fact that we invent new ways of creating value and delivering work doesn't change the basic concept of the organization. And we will still need to conceptualize the relationship of all of these dimensions using an organizational model.

The Front/Back Organization Model

The most complex organization forms result from closely and loosely related operating frameworks (columns 2 and 3 in the operating framework continuum). These tend to have all basic structures at play: product and service lines, geographic markets, customer segments, and business functions. While the parts are largely the same, the ways in which they are wired together result in different leadership behaviors and business outcomes.

Many global companies use what we call a "front/back" organization model for closely and loosely related portfolios to get the right balance of local autonomy and speed, and enterprise leverage and scale. Jay Galbraith first described this construct in the 1990s (Galbraith, 1995). Our experience working with the leadership teams of dozens of global companies over the past twenty-five years has confirmed that the font/back model is even more relevant in the 2020s for global companies with multiple product, service, technology, and solutions offerings.

Conceptualizing the relationships within a closely or loosely related portfolio is not easy work. We find that using the front/back construct allows a design team to articulate assumptions about power dynamics in the organization in a non-hierarchical way. Every part of the organization has a unique and significant part to play in defining and executing strategy. The model makes this clear.

From this core model, we can strip away or add parts and connect them in a variety of ways to drive different accountabilities and behaviors. Building the organization model helps us understand where we are today based on decisions made in the past and where we want to adjust for the future. In this way, the design work focuses on relationships and accountability, something that mere changes to an organization chart cannot do.

Virtually every business contains the three major components of work represented in the basic front/back model (Figure 3.3). Let's look more closely at each.

Figure 3.3 Basic front/back organization model

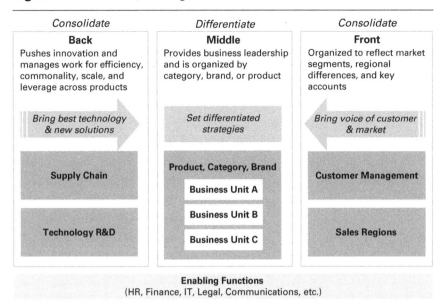

The "front" is typically the customer-facing components of the organization. These may include all manner of sales channels, customer marketing, product localization, solutions integration, and customer service. The front-end of organizations used to be fairly simple. Sales organizations tended to be geographically organized. And if you went to market business-to-business and wanted to be customer-centric, you might have organized the front by vertical (industry). But today, many companies operate in complex ecosystems where customers are also competitors. For example, SpartanNash, an $8 billion, food distribution and supermarket chain operating in the American Midwest, had a fairly simple core retail business. But when Amazon moved into fresh grocery delivery, they became both a customer and a competitor, complicating decision-making in the front-end sales channels.

Further, for companies that are trying to execute on solution strategies, the front takes on the accountability to bundle, integrate, and price the firm's offerings as it goes to market. So-called *solution* architects are new roles that bring together all the value identified by the sales and account managers. Then *delivery* architects orchestrate the implementation of these complex projects.

In the business-to-consumer space, channels have become more complex. It is not uncommon for consumer goods companies to have wholesale partners, their own retail stores, and direct-to-consumer e-commerce sales. How these channels work together to deliver a seamless customer experience in an integrated marketplace typically falls on the groups in the front of the organization to manage.

The "middle" owns the business strategy and development of the offering, whether a product, service, brand, or category. The middle is designed to focus on differentiated strategies. The question to ask is: Does each of the units in the middle have a unique set of competitors and/or customers that would require a differentiated strategy? If so, then each group in the middle requires some autonomy and focus. This naturally leads to good discussion of what work each unit in the middle needs to control fully and what can be shared, and the assumptions for commonality. Often, product development and product marketing sit in these units. But, then the next level of design can focus on to what degree should engineering, operations, manufacturing, or research be shared or dedicated?

With a differentiated middle, portfolio management becomes an important leadership discussion. While innovation often springs from small experiments, real growth comes from identifying the winners and investing differentially in them. It is rare that all units in the middle are in the same stage of growth or maturity. The success of the closely and loosely related portfolio operating model depends not only on the leadership of each product unit, but also on the collective ability of leadership to make hard choices regarding investment and resource allocation across the units.

The "back" houses essential expertise that creates and delivers the offering profitably. We say these groups are in the back because, from a customer viewpoint, these groups are often not visible externally. However, the terminology is not intended to reduce their significance. Typical back-end groups are core engineering, operations, supply chain, manufacturing, technology platforms, research, and data and analytics. Because this expertise is expensive to obtain or requires intense capital investment, this work is often consolidated so that it can be leveraged across the various product units. Here the design questions include: Where can we have common processes and systems? Where can we pool resources and where do we need to dedicate them? How do we best make trade-offs when capacity is limited?

It is this stage that the idea of Enterprise Roles becomes important. As the model is developed, these roles document assumptions regarding accountabilities and decision making for each part of the organization. Figure 3.4 provides an example of accountabilities for the core roles of each part of an organization.

Figure 3.4 Enterprise roles example

Back: Platforms	Middle: Categories	Front: Go-to-Market Units
Builds platforms for efficiency, commonality, scale, and leverage across categories.	Develops market-leading assets that can be configured into customer-specific solutions	Coordinates how we prioritize value creation in the market, and bundles solutions across the platforms for customers.
• Delivers scaled services and assures compliance to protect enterprise interests. • Creates functional plans to build critical capabilities to execute the company growth strategy. • Manages technology roadmaps and builds infrastructure in line with growth plans. • Enables success of business objectives through oversight of functional resource pools, effective process, and best practices. Manages central operational functions, where it makes sense. • Sets a cost envelope for the function.	• Identifies long-term market and technology trends. Sets growth, margin, and cash objectives. • Defines replicable, integrated solutions that meet customer needs profitably. • Aligns components to deliver profitable integrated solutions. • Manages development programs. Assures activation of new offerings in the market, including effective launch and customer support standards. • Sets pricing guidelines and service standards. Collaborates with go-to-market units to set growth targets for each. • Manages delivery of all solutions to customers across the value stream.	• Sets account and market segment growth strategies and plans. • Designs and integrates solutions for buyer groups. • Sets commercial strategy and plans for buyer groups. • Configures profitable solution sets for each account, based on solution sets provided by categories. Sets tactical pricing. • Owns the P&L across the offerings. • Ensures customer commitments are fully met, working with platforms and categories units. • Brings customer intelligence to categories to inform new product development and growth targets.

Variations on the Front/Back Model

There are three core variations of the basic model which create combinations that cover many global business strategies. We offer them here as a useful starting point for customizing a model for your own business.

Variation A: Differentiated Middle with Consolidated Front and Back

In many companies, the basic organizational model is a set of product lines in the middle that each leverage a shared front-end and a shared back-end, much like the generic model. The conditions for this model are:

- The middle is a set of differentiated products or services that require some autonomy in order to innovate and compete in their own market niche.
- These product lines can leverage shared expertise or platforms to create competitive advantage and therefore the back-end functions can be shared, at least to some degree.
- Customers not only buy across product lines, but also want bundled or integrated offerings. The groups in the front must be able to work agnostically across the product lines.

Take Microsoft as an example, shown in a simplified model in Figure 3.5. The middle segment is organized into product groups, currently Productivity and Business Processes (Office 365/Teams, Dynamics, and LinkedIn), Intelligent Cloud (Azure), and Personal Computing (Windows, Xbox, Surface, and Search). These are the key points of agility and differentiation— each product group is focused on a unique offering and has a unique set of competitors. The customer-facing front end—sales, customer management, and a large services consulting organization—is shared across the product groups. And likewise, the back end, which is all about artificial intelligence, machine learning, and cloud capabilities, is now the foundation that powers all Microsoft offerings.

Figure 3.5 Microsoft 2020 simplified organization model

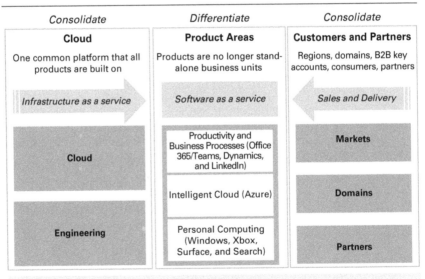

Consolidate	Differentiate	Consolidate
Cloud	**Product Areas**	**Customers and Partners**
One common platform that all products are built on	Products are no longer stand-alone business units	Regions, domains, B2B key accounts, consumers, partners
Infrastructure as a service	*Software as a service*	*Sales and Delivery*
Cloud	Productivity and Business Processes (Office 365/Teams, Dynamics, and LinkedIn)	**Markets**
	Intelligent Cloud (Azure)	**Domains**
Engineering	Personal Computing (Windows, Xbox, Surface, and Search)	**Partners**

Enabling Functions
(HR, Finance, IT, Legal, Communications, etc.)

Variation B: Differentiated Middle and Back with a Shared Front

In other companies, the back-end is strongly connected to the middle rather than consolidated and shared. The conditions for this are:

- The products or services in the middle are so differentiated that they require their own unique configuration of "back-end" expertise.

- However, customers may buy across product lines and may also want bundled or integrated offerings, requiring the maintenance of a shared front end.

In this variation, we commonly see functions such as supply chain or systems developers closely aligned to the product managers and even managed by or sharing a reporting structure with the product groups. The rationale of combining the back and middle around the product lines is that there is little leverage to be gained by more centrally managed functions because the supply chain or the technologies associated with each product are quite diverse or even unique to each business.

The customer-facing front-end, however, can be pooled or shared by all the businesses under a single commercial reporting structure because the products are serving the same customers. This front-end is built for scale—leveraging customer relationships, as in Variation A.

The medical device industry has been evolving along this pattern for some time. Figure 3.6 is an amalgam of over a dozen global companies we have worked with in this sector. What was a fairly simple hardware business has evolved into three distinct product offerings in many of these companies—hardware devices, disposables and supplies, and software and integrated medical data. The supply chains and innovation processes for each of these offerings is highly differentiated. Little cost efficiency is gained from pooling them all together, so such capabilities are best attached to the product groups to provide the benefits of innovation and speed.

However, the customer in the medical device industry does not think in terms of hardware, supplies, or software. The customer is a specialty-oriented physician who wonders, "What thoracic surgical solution can you provide that will give me the best outcome in the operating room?" And, the customer is also a hospital system procurement manager who asks, "What solution can you provide that will reduce readmissions, be cost-efficient to maintain, and will integrate with our existing systems?" Therefore, the front-end must be designed around customer segments that cut across product offerings.

Figure 3.6 Medical device company example

Differentiate		Consolidate

Product Innovation	**Business Leadership**	**Market Access and Delivery**
Pushes innovation and manages work for efficiency, commonality, scale, and leverage within products	Provides full life cycle management across a set of differentiated products	Organized to configure solutions within markets

Bring best technology & new solutions →	*Manage fully loaded business units*	← *Bring voice of customer & market*

Devices, Hardware
Engineering, Supply Chain, Operations, Product Marketing

Disposables and Supplies
Engineering, Supply Chain, Operations, Product Marketing

Software and Services
Engineering, Supply Chain, Operations, Product Marketing

Practice Marketing | Customer Marketing | Buyer/Payer Marketing

Region

Countries

Key Accounts

Enabling Functions
(HR, Finance, IT, Legal, Communications, etc.)

Variation C: Differentiated Front and Middle with Shared Back

In this model, the products or services in the middle are connected to their own customer-facing teams in the front-end. The conditions for this are:

- Customer segments largely line up with the product offering and customers do not purchase across product lines.

- Products can be built on a common platform, and leveraging this proprietary expertise and asset is core to the business strategy.

3M, illustrated in Figure 3.7, is a classic example of a business built on this organization model. Like Gore, 3M centers on a handful of core technologies common to all products, in this case adhesives and non-woven fabrics. In fact, the company chooses what products to offer based on their connection to those technologies. But the industries that 3M sells into are quite different, requiring each product group to have a specialized sales and marketing organization to meet the needs of diverse corporate and consumer customers.

Figure 3.7 3M 2020 simplified organization model

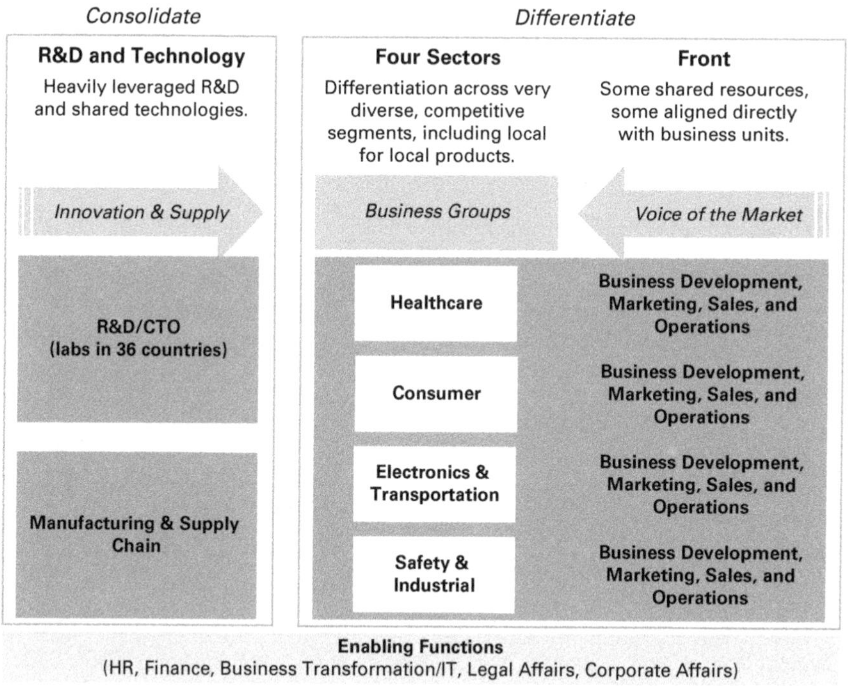

Consolidate	Differentiate	
R&D and Technology	**Four Sectors**	**Front**
Heavily leveraged R&D and shared technologies.	Differentiation across very diverse, competitive segments, including local for local products.	Some shared resources, some aligned directly with business units.
Innovation & Supply	*Business Groups*	*Voice of the Market*
R&D/CTO (labs in 36 countries)	**Healthcare**	**Business Development, Marketing, Sales, and Operations**
	Consumer	**Business Development, Marketing, Sales, and Operations**
Manufacturing & Supply Chain	**Electronics & Transportation**	**Business Development, Marketing, Sales, and Operations**
	Safety & Industrial	**Business Development, Marketing, Sales, and Operations**

Enabling Functions
(HR, Finance, Business Transformation/IT, Legal Affairs, Corporate Affairs)

For all these variations, the design of the product teams in the middle can be constructed in a variety of ways that reflect how different they are from one another and how much autonomy each requires to compete in its unique market space. A continuum is shown in Table 3.1.

Where Does the P&L Go?

Assigning P&L responsibility to a general manager is a common means of establishing clear accountability for a product or service line. Business leaders naturally want their scope of authority to match their assigned accountability, and many top executives, including CEOs, are drawn to these models of accountability. A common assumption is that the P&L sits in the *middle* of the front/back organization model. In the closely-related portfolio, this often leads to simplistic over-use of fully loaded, heavyweight product teams that operate independently, when in fact they should be leveraging more of the assets of the enterprise. This mismatch creates the perception of accountability.

Table 3.1 Types of teams in the "middle"

	Light-Weight Product Teams	Middle-Weight Product Teams	Heavy-Weight Business Units
Typical Functions Embedded in the Team	Strategy, innovation, product planning	Strategy, innovation, product planning, product management, product development team management, consumer marketing	Strategy, innovation, product planning, life cycle management, product development, consumer marketing, regulatory, quality, sales channel strategy
Typical Team Leader and Metrics	Product Manager: revenue, sales support	General Manager or Product Leader: revenue, some shadow P&L elements	General Manager: P&L for revenue and gross margin, customer metrics
Typical Reporting Level	Into a marketing or product management leader	Into a division head or group product management executive	Into the CEO, COO, Group or Sector President
Focus of Priorities	Drive new technology strategy and big-bet initiatives	Drive global strategy and product/service plans. Product development, life-cycle management, and marketing	Oversee all elements of the strategy, offering, marketing, with guidance to supply chain and commercial support
Examples	Google (product areas for consumer applications)	Gore PepsiCo Kellogg's	General Mills Philips

But, not only do these organizations have higher cost structures with a great deal of duplication and unrewarded complexity, very often they conflict with the need for more boundary-spanning ways of working. Recall our discussion of enterprise agility in Chapter 1 in contrast to the agility that is created by small business units and autonomous teams. Hardened P&Ls in heavyweight business units that "own" their own engineering, supply chain management, staff support, and other functions often create a false sense of agility.

Building an organization model with the front/back framework is an effective way to challenge leadership to reconsider conventional thinking about P&L. By working through the options, it often becomes apparent that alternatives exist with shared front and back resource teams that can bring greater cost effectiveness and scale while retaining agility in the middle.

The front/back organization model also exposes the increasing likelihood in today's customer-focused organizations that the P&L belongs in the *front* of the model, not the middle. Companies that are bundling solutions across multiple product and service components, similar to the medical devices example, are shifting P&L accountability to customer-facing geographies and account management teams. Accenture's operating model, realigned in 2020, shifted primary P&L responsibility from global operating groups to regional market units in order to enable the customization of complex, cross-services solutions to clients.

The role that any given product line plays in the greater portfolio is another consideration that should force a more critical review of P&Ls in the middle. For example, "winning" for one of the product lines might not mean profitability. This product line may provide an important component to the full solution but, standing alone, may not be a viable profit engine. Or, another product line may be critical for brand building and holding market share. P&L ownership becomes less of a source of tension and focus when each part of the organization knows its contribution, respects the contribution of the others, and is measured and rewarded for the collective success.

Organization Models Below the Enterprise Layer

We have been looking at the alignment of organization model to operating framework at the enterprise level. The same patterns hold as you design levels below the top layer.

Let's go back to Gore. As we described above, the company at the enterprise level deliberately only connected and leveraged a few assets—core technology, business function expertise, and enabling function efficiency. The three business divisions retained a fair amount of control over product development, marketing, sales, and manufacturing resources.

Figure 3.8 The front/back model for Gore Medical Products

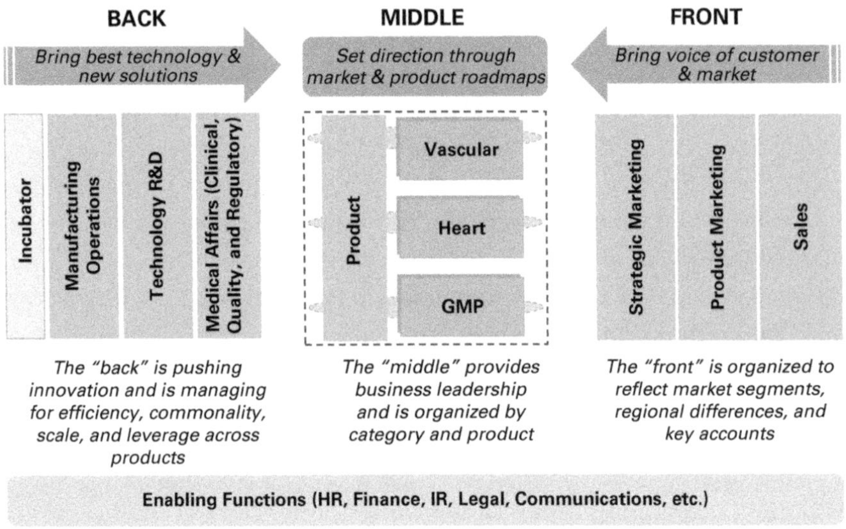
BACK
MIDDLE
FRONT
Bring best technology & new solutions
Set direction through market & product roadmaps
Bring voice of customer & market
Incubator
Manufacturing Operations
Technology R&D
Medical Affairs (Clinical, Quality, and Regulatory)
Product
Vascular
Heart
GMP
Strategic Marketing
Product Marketing
Sales
The "back" is pushing innovation and is managing for efficiency, commonality, scale, and leverage across products
The "middle" provides business leadership and is organized by category and product
The "front" is organized to reflect market segments, regional differences, and key accounts
Enabling Functions (HR, Finance, IR, Legal, Communications, etc.)

The Medical Division, however, is run as a *closely related* set of product lines focused on heart and vascular products. The category leaders in the middle set strategies and teams are assembled around priorities in a process that involves all parts of the division. Back-end resources are pooled for scale so the deployment of this expertise and capacity has to be carefully considered. The front-end is also completely consolidated as customers (typically hospitals and governments) buy across the product offering. Figure 3.8 shows the front/back model for Gore Medical Products.

The power of aligning organization model to operating framework is that this work allows each part of the global company to be designed fit for purpose within a consistent logic that reflects the business strategy. As conditions change, leaders can proactively make targeted adjustments to reflect market shifts or drive different employee or customer behaviors. Operating framework and organization model thinking allows for deliberate and dynamic design of the organization.

The Design Process

Creating an organization model is strategic work and should be led and owned by the most senior leaders in the organization unit under consideration.

We find that the design work is enhanced when this top team is augmented by participants from a level or two below. People in these roles are closer to the current realities of the work and help push for change. We suggest that our clients include high-influence, high-potential systems thinkers who sit in pivotal roles in the current organization in this work, as well as a few that are fairly new and bring relevant external perspectives.

The top team must be part of the work because they have to commit to the direction and lead the organization forward (even though their own roles may change as a result of the design process). If you only have the top team, however, they may convince themselves that the status quo is not so bad. The next layer is included to keep things real—to push for change and bring the voice of the broader organization into the work.

Before this design team starts imagining the future together, four foundational "business case and discovery" activities should be completed:

1 Clarification of the strategic priorities with alignment on how "we will win."

2 Identification of the short list of organization capabilities (new muscles) that articulate what the organizational must be able to do together to deliver on the strategy.

3 Current-state diagnostic providing an honest picture of gaps against ambitions.

4 Operating framework discussion to surface and align assumptions of how closely connected the current and future product portfolio should be, and where integration adds value and where it does not.

In addition, we find that a few questions focused on the work are excellent catalysts for helping a group develop organization model options:

1 Idea to product: How will we develop products faster in the new model? What role does each part of the organization play in innovation and execution?

2 Demand generation: How will the new model help us gain customers and expand into new geographies and channels?

3 Delivery and service: How will this model help us go to market as one company and deliver a consistent customer experience, where we need to?

Remember that different organization charts can support the same organization model. The organization chart is largely unconnected to the organization model. Size of leadership team, scope of roles, reporting relationships, spans of control, and number of layers are tactical decisions made *after* the organization model is agreed upon.

In sum, look to consolidate where scale gives advantage—cost, expertise, global reach, platforms, technology investments. Differentiate where autonomy gives advantage—product innovation, customer knowledge, go-to-market relevance. Use this logic as you design each component and each layer of the organization to yield a creative, thoughtful, and efficient design process.

Key Takeaways

- The organization model is a graphic depiction of design concepts that helps to make the invisible, abstract concept that is "organization" tangible to a design team.

- The front/back model is a useful way to show, in a non-hierarchical way, the relationship between commercial, product, and operations parts of the organization.

- Enterprise roles lay out the accountabilities for the major parts of the organization model.

- Organization models should be developed for each unit of the company and are a critical design step before the creation of organization charts.

References

Galbraith, J R (1995) *Designing Organizations: An executive briefing on strategy, structure, and process*, Jossey-Bass, San Francisco

Harari, Y N (2015) *Sapiens: A brief history of humankind*, Harper, New York

Kesler, G and Kates, A (2011) *Leading Organization Design: How to make organization design decisions to drive the results you want*, Jossey-Bass, San Francisco

The Vertical Organization 04

The magic that happens when human beings think and act together is why we have organizations. Organizations exist to allow us to make complex decisions. They help us process information, experience, and insight in ways that individuals and machines cannot do on their own. Artificial intelligence and smart machines will augment our collective decision-making ability but won't fully replace it any time soon.

As we sit at our homes in New York, Connecticut, and Florida in the United States during 2020 writing this book, the world is responding to the Coronavirus pandemic. Governments, companies, and hospitals are scrambling to get people and supplies to the right places at the right time as the virus moves across the globe. Amid the heroics of individuals and stories of businesses pivoting their production priorities is a general sense of disappointment. Surely, our governments had plans for a crisis such as this, didn't they? We might not expect to have all the masks or ventilators needed on hand, but we would expect there were plans for how we could make them quickly. That there would be plans for how we would coordinate across hospital systems, state lines, and national boundaries. That even at a time of ambiguity regarding how best to slow the virus, our leaders would have mechanisms to make consistent and aligned decisions regarding testing, social distancing, business closures, and mask wearing. And, that they would communicate their reasoning clearly.

We often say that the organizations that make faster, better decisions win. Fast decisions are required because a good decision that isn't timely loses value. But a quick decision that doesn't consider full data and consequences across stakeholders and time horizons will look foolish soon enough. Typically, when we talk about organizational decision-making, it is in the context of getting products launched, making capital investments, or moving into new markets. A poor decision means lost revenue. Unfortunately, what we are witnessing on a global scale with Coronavirus is poor decisions resulting in lost lives and livelihoods.

In this chapter, we will examine the role and design of the vertical organization. We'll argue that the best way to create a system that can move fast in a coordinated manner, empower innovation and action against a collective goal, and adapt quickly to change is one that is built on a set of clear leadership layers. When each layer is designed to make a unique contribution to decisions, and roles are connected through well-designed mechanisms to move information to the right place within the organization, the organization can move with speed. We will cover:

- a new way to think about hierarchy
- how to design a system of interlocking leadership layers
- the relationship of individual role design to leadership layers

Why Hierarchy Shouldn't be a Bad Word

Perhaps there is no greater shibboleth in organization design than the idea of hierarchy. If one wants to sound current and forward thinking in 2020, then denouncing the evils of hierarchy is the quickest way to signal you are at the vanguard.

Hierarchy is often used as a proxy for "rigid." The term is used to suggest an organization in which information only moves up and down through a strict chain of command. An organization where variation and innovation are stifled at the front line. An organization of silos where people cannot work across unit lines without permission from above. And, for sure, the first dictionary definition of hierarchy is "a system or organization in which people or groups are ranked one above the other according to status or authority" (Hobson, 2004).

Most companies we work with have long sought to move away from running their company in this "hierarchical" way. For decades, leaders have embraced the idea that strong and purposeful horizontal ways of working are important. Connecting across boundaries is simply the way that work needs to get done today in complex, multi-dimensional organizations.

Yet, while these same companies may have moved beyond layers of supervisors sending out commands and checking work at multiple levels, the truth is that, even in 2020, many leaders who see themselves as quite progressive are still struggling to build the nimble, flexible organizations that they know are needed to compete effectively. It is easy to find evidence that a company has an unproductive and old-fashioned hierarchy. In these companies, leaders haven't divorced status from titles and pay from number of people managed. They have unwritten codes that say you don't meet with your boss's peer if your boss isn't also in the meeting. Leaders may manage multimillion-dollar budgets but must get signoffs from above to make a $10,000 investment. And, too often, the "senior leadership team" is limited to vice presidents or some other arbitrary level, rather than comprised of the right roles that can best contribute to the discussion at hand.

This all needs to be addressed. But, simply blaming hierarchy as the culprit is simplistic. In fact, many of these common issues need to be and can be addressed by changes to management processes, leadership behavioral expectations, human resource systems, and metrics.

So then, when is hierarchy a good thing? The other definition of hierarchy is "an arrangement or classification of things according to relative importance or inclusiveness" (Hobson, 2004). With this reframing, we have a term that helps us think about how we group work in various layers, specifically the work of leaders.

It is productive to think about hierarchy as a way to differentiate thought and focus. Steve Drotter pointed out that in a well-designed hierarchy of leadership, each leader does not just do a bigger version of the work of the leader below. Rather, at each layer there should be a change in time horizon, time allocation, and complexity of problems to solve (Drotter, 2011).

This idea of a hierarchy of thought and focus, and of differential velocity at various layers of leadership, ensures that each layer makes a unique contribution to the work of the organization. And it gets us out of the old definition of hierarchy based on status. In fact, we will see that when we start to look at how work at the top of the organization is measured by how well it empowers the base of the organization, we can build the backbone of an organization that can be agile and adaptive as well as coordinated and connected.

Going forward, we will use the term "vertical organization" to avoid confusion with the common definition of hierarchy and the negative connotations of the word.

What Happens When We Don't Design the Vertical Organization?

Across the hundreds of organization assessments that we have conducted over 20 years, a number of common themes emerge as frustrations. Three can be traced directly to poorly designed vertical organizations.

Decisions Are Made at Too High a Level

We often hear from senior leaders that they are exasperated by the passivity of their direct reports—not in the reports' individual roles as managers of their respective teams, but as a collective group. A typical comment might be, "They are quick to tell us what isn't working. But why don't they just get together and fix it? They have big jobs and they are making good money. No one has told them they can't address the problems they see. But they don't step up or take action."

Yet, those same direct reports often claim that they are disempowered. And, it is quite rational for them not to act. They do not see any reward or incentive to self-organize with peers to initiate the work required to solve systemic issues—and certainly not to try to do so alone. Further, those that see issues often don't have the information or the mechanisms to coordinate effectively with each other, and they might lack the strategic perspective to make smart trade-offs. It is usually safer to check with those more senior, to ask for permission. So, work and decisions tend to move upward in the organization.

Contributing to this dynamic are senior leaders who like making operational decisions. This is particularly true in fast-growing organizations where complexity has grown faster than leadership capability. And when great operators and functional wizards have been promoted into roles that require longer-term, strategic thinking. The senior level may complain that the decisions land in their lap, but they continue to make them.

Duplication of Work and Effort

When each layer fails to have a unique role, the same work and decisions get made multiple times. The root cause of this issue is often that layers have been added to solve career progression issues rather than being designed around needed work. "Assistant" and "senior" levels are added to promote people, pay them more, or give them supervisory experience. This is where outmoded human resource systems actually encourage hierarchy in the negative sense of the word. Rather than find creative ways to develop and reward people, layers are shoe-horned into the organization to work around reward or pay-grade limitations. Work is not redesigned.

What we typically see here is that people in these new layers become "checkers, checking on the checkers below." A typical organization assessment comment is, "I feel like a mailbox. I collect data from below and pass it up. And, I cascade information and programs down without adding a whole lot of value." Certainly not the picture of a lean, agile organization.

Organizational Units Are Not Designed to Connect

The third common issue that can be traced to a poorly designed vertical organization is that each organizational unit is optimized without consideration of how roles will connect with peers horizontally. Each leader designs their group in a vacuum with their own mix of roles focused on product and service development, interface management, shared services, and delivery operations. And in isolation, these designs often do make sense.

But then when we try to connect marketers, or engineers, or data scientists across units formally or informally, we find that role descriptions and expectations are not aligned. From one assessment:

> I thought it should be fairly easy to find all our project managers and start creating a community. But I quickly realized that we weren't defining the work the same way or even knew who was doing it. Beyond using different methodologies, we each had our own management structures and ways of working. What looked like an easy move to start sharing project management resources was made much more difficult by the variety we had each built in the design of our groups. And the variation wasn't because the work was so different. It was just that we hadn't coordinated when we designed the roles.

We will now show how to create a classification of leadership work, with each layer inclusive of the work below but not duplicating it.

Designing the Vertical Organization

The terms authority, accountability, and responsibility are key words in the vertical organization, but they are often used interchangeably. We will clarify some definitions that build on A G L Romme's (2019) distinctions:

Authority: Authority determines the boundaries and scope of decisions you can make, typically regarding how resources are deployed, the amount of money you can spend, the people you can hire, and the processes and systems you can use and change.

Authority is typically a vertical construct in that each layer has a broader scope of authority (e.g., budgets become bigger as one moves up a layer). Often, when levels of authority are set too low, we see the frustration of leaders in big jobs having to ask for permission to act from above.

Authority can also play out horizontally when peers have a veto. For example, IT, legal, security, risk management, brand, and finance are roles that can often veto peer decisions if they fall outside of preset parameters. The design of decision processes—including clear boundaries—helps to remove these unwelcome surprises.

Accountability: Accountability sets out the expectations of how your performance is judged. It is determined externally by others in the organization. This is what your role is expected to deliver and contribute. When accountabilities are unclear, people may do work that overlaps with others or try to make decisions that others see as their own.

Responsibility: Responsibility is an intrinsic motivation. It is expressed through discretionary effort—going above and beyond. If accountability is set externally—"Here is what we need from you in this role"—responsibility is the internal force that pushes people to perform with excellence and to proactively suggest innovations and process improvements and identify risks. It is enhanced through shared purpose and values.

The design of the vertical organization is essentially the design of roles, power dynamics, decision rights, and management and reward systems to create the right mix of authority, accountability, and responsibility not just in individuals, but also in whole layers of leadership.

In many organizations, however, the layers of leadership are used primarily as a cascade mechanism for information to be transmitted from the top rather than each owning their own unique work. The result is that hierarchical relationships become a source of unhealthy tension and complexity. "If I am not a direct report to the leader, or I am layered, then I am out of the conversation. I am not a player anymore, just a conduit."

It is impossible to fully divorce reporting relationships from this discussion. However, by focusing on the work of each layer and then identifying

Figure 4.1 Layers of leadership work

Strategic Leadership Layer

- Set the vision, manage the portfolio, set clear direction, priorities, and culture
- Make big bet and trade-off decisions
- Communicate purpose with one voice

Time horizon: 5–10 Years

Integrative Leadership Layer

- Manage the forums, systems, processes, and ways of working to drive horizontal, structured collaboration across boundaries

Time horizon: 2–5 Years

Anchor Business Layer (Operating Layer)

- Serve customers profitably
- Enable teams with direction, resources, coaching, and clarity—consistent with enterprise guidance

Time horizon: 12–24 Months

the right roles and perspectives for each conversation, you can create a logic that reflects the work rather than the status of reporting lines.

Figure 4.1 shows the three core layers of leadership in an organization. While this construct may not apply to very small organizations, the same thought process and questions can be scaled up or down to almost any size organization in which you have multiple layers of leaders.

Strategic Layer

The strategic layer should be making a small set of big decisions. We like the idea of "differential velocity." This team often needs to slow down and spend significant time together listening and looking at trends and options. Their agenda should be to focus on a few high-impact outcomes. The decisions of this group should be informed by broad input from internal and external voices, and that takes time. When all members of this layer are aligned, the rest of the organization can move fast.

The strategic layer can be as simple as the direct reports to the top leader. But because these reporting relationships are often somewhat arbitrary, the strategic layer is better thought of as the collection of roles that together represent all the components of the enterprise. The symbolism of who sits in the strategic layer is important to consider. All areas of the company should see their voice represented in some way.

For example, one of our large clients has a global executive committee (GEC) of nearly 40 roles. Three of these roles are rotational, to bring account management voices from the two-dozen market units into strategic decision-making. From a hierarchical standpoint, these roles are a layer or two below the other GEC members, but their presence at the table is an acknowledgement of their pivotal place in the organization.

In this same company, the CEO has established an informal "kitchen cabinet" of just seven roles that often comes together to make decisions after input and debate by the GEC.

The typical core work of the strategic layer (for an enterprise) includes:

- setting the business model (how we make money), operating model (how we manage the company), and boundaries (core values, culture, leadership expectations)
- endorsing the vision for the company
- defining company risk profile, managing risk, and ensuring "right-to-operate" compliance
- ensuring company leadership continuity and viability
- setting the corporate growth strategy
- allocating capital across the investment portfolio
- establishing annual targets within the context of the growth plan

Integrative Layer

The integrative layer is often overlooked, yet so powerful when well designed. These are the senior leaders with big jobs, usually two and three levels down from the top. There is work they perform as individuals, and there is work they must do together. It is this latter work that they are often unclear about. What should we accomplish as a team when we come together? This question assumes there are even forums in place for this layer to connect in a meaningful way.

When harnessed purposefully, this is the layer that makes the complex machinery of the organization work effectively. Together, these leaders decide where to drive harmonized processes and where to allow localization and autonomy. They model collaboration and create and champion the ways of work that drive the culture. They make the connections at the boundaries of product and service lines, markets, and functions that create value for customers. This layer includes staff leaders as well as operators.

The more closely related the portfolio of work, the more that the integrative layer needs to spend time together building relationships and working on their unique set of topics. These are the people that jointly lead teams across borders (skills, time zones, organization jurisdiction) to solve problems, amplify innovations, and create customer solutions.

Most companies have no shortage of best practices. But these practices often remain invisible outside the unit using them. There is nothing sadder than when an executive in a meeting with colleagues hears a story and says, "I didn't know we were doing that already." One of the potential benefits of scale is the ability to leverage the skills, ideas, and experience that are available across the enterprise. The integrative layer is a critical mechanism for scale. When it is missing or underutilized, this the place where the good intentions of the matrix often fail.

The success of collaborative relationships and decision mechanisms across the integrative layer sets the tone for the rest of the organization. The typical core work of the integrative layer (for an enterprise) includes:

- make recommendations on company direction choices
- define enterprise initiatives and operating priorities within the context of the growth plan
- sponsor innovation initiatives and new capability development
- monitor cross-boundary performance and make cross-unit trade-off decisions
- define organizational arrangements for execution of the strategy
- align resource levels for key growth and client priorities
- manage operating-level talent for growth

Operational Layer

The operational layer in the large multi-dimensional company can be thought of as the "anchor layer" for running the business day-to-day, the center of gravity. This is where the action is, close to the customer. These operating units should be delegated substantial authority to serve customers profitably. For example, the leaders who control product mix and margin targets often sit at this layer.

The leaders in the operational anchor layer execute within the boundaries and guidance provided by the senior layers. Critically, this means that the executives in the integrative and strategic layers are not running the business day-to-day. Rather, their role is to create an environment for these operating teams to win. The strategic and integrative layers empower the anchor layer by setting clear boundaries and priorities of the firm and then providing the freedom to act within those boundaries.

Now you have a system of leadership layers; a hierarchy of focus and thought that adds unique value. Here, senior leaders work in service of the anchor layer, providing the operators with the direction, guardrails, and resources to move nimbly on the ground.

In this system, authority and accountability can be specified in a way that motivates collaboration and responsibility.

For example, consider a company that produces cosmetic products. The company wins in the marketplace by closely following trends and getting new products out faster than competitors. The strategic layer is comprised of the key functional leaders—product, supply chain, marketing, merchandising, brand, retail operations, HR, legal, finance, and the heads of North America, Europe, and Emerging Markets. The integrative layer is the functional staff across the three regions. The operating layer is the product category teams—nails, hair, lips, eyes, skincare, face.

Speed-to-market is critically important in this business. So, each product category team has been delegated the *authority* to determine whether to use in-house or third party laboratories to develop and test new products. The product teams are *accountable* for volume growth, margin, and for meeting launch schedules for their category. These targets are set by the strategic layer as part of the planning process.

The real prospects for growth in this business are highly profitable kits: holiday-themed packages, travel retail offers, and celebrity-endorsed collections. These kits require variations to product design and packaging and often must be delivered under tight timelines. To select the best opportunities and design, package, and market these kits across the category teams and functional groups requires a high degree of coordination. Many choices must be made, and talent has to be shared. The success of these projects often comes down to the discretionary effort that the teams make when on these special projects. Motivating this *responsibility* is the work of the integrative layer. The integrative layer's role here is to create shared purpose and instill confidence that they are working together to help these project teams succeed.

Connecting the Layers Together

To work as a system, the layers need a sophisticated rhythm of conversations up and down. This is quite different from the simple cascade of information from the top or the occasional taskforce inviting some upward input. The concept of leadership layers is not about creating new, hard boundaries. It is about creating clarity of focus when people come together. This is especially important because in one forum a role may be part of the strategic layer and in a different forum focused on integrative work.

Let's go back to the cosmetics company. The regional and business function executives are part of the strategic layer when they come together with corporate staff to set the enterprise strategy. However, in the demand planning cycle, these executives would be part of the integrative layer together with a layer below. They own the business forecast as well as broad resource decisions. They take part in a set of planning meetings held at a regular cadence to review forecast data and solve capacity and resource allocation issues across the product teams. In their integrative role, they work together to ensure close partnerships at the anchor layer below them across global market and product categories. The anchor layer is where specific strategies for "how we will win together" are set. These teams of market and product own their business plans jointly and are delegated responsibility for results. We call this planning and review cadence the "business handshake" (Kesler and Kates, 2016).

This approach also allows for a more effective way to think about decision rights. Dotted and solid lines become irrelevant. Dual reporting is the norm; some members sit on two teams of equal importance. For high-value decisions that must be made collaboratively across organizational boundaries, well-designed forums ensure the right conversations and promote structured collaboration. Table 4.1 provides an example of forums at the strategic and integrative layer for a large services company.

Table 4.1 Strategic and integrative layers example

Purpose	Work	Forums	Cadence
Enterprise Direction	• Set the business model (how we make money), operating model (how we manage the company), and boundaries (core values, culture, leadership expectations) • Define company risk profile, manage risk, and ensure compliance • Ensure company leadership continuity and viability	Executive Committee (CEO and Direct Reports)	Monthly
Growth and Investment Plan	• Set the corporate growth strategy • Allocate capital across the investment portfolio • Establish annual targets within the context of the growth plan	Operating Committee (Subset of CEO Direct Reports including Chief Strategy Officer, CFO, and CHRO)	Annually with Quarterly Updates
Organization Integration and Management	• Define enterprise initiations and operating priorities within the context of the growth plan and annual goals • Provide input to strategy regarding client, market, and technology trends • Sponsor innovation initiatives and new capabilities • Monitor cross-boundary performance and make cross-unit trade-off decisions • Define organization arrangements for execution of the strategy and priorities • Manage operating level talent for growth	Management Committee (Executive Committee plus another 20 key global roles)	Quarterly

| Demand Planning | • Review, debate, and endorse forecast data from center and local leadership
• Analyze and align around resource levels for key growth and client priorities
• Integrate capabilities and capacity requirements across the geography and service lines | Planning Committee (Subset of Management Committee including Marketing and Operations) | Monthly |

Role Design

Thoughtful role design is an important component of the vertical organization. As part of our organization design work, we frequently focus on those roles that are pivotal to new strategies, are critical for connecting across organizational boundaries, or are new and not well understood. We help to create "real role descriptions" that highlight the contribution of the role, measures of success, decision authority, time horizons for focus and time allocation, and the high trust vertical and lateral relationships that will need to be built. We find that this kind of role design helps to communicate expectations and match motivation and competencies to the work. Figure 4.2 shows a one-page role description. With this format, one can quickly ensure that roles stacked in a job family at the global (strategic), regional (integrative), and market (operational) layers are differentiated appropriately.

For example, consider a global company that serves as a third-party implementer of software systems. One of the major products they support is called ABS software. Thinking of roles in terms of layers not only helps spell out accountabilities, it also helps to make clear what decisions and activities a role should *not* be involved in.

The global ABS lead is accountable for global strategy, thought leadership, alliances, offerings, solution standard, campaigns, large initiatives, and capability development. The global ABS lead supports large cross-border sales opportunities as a senior representative of the company. This role does not conduct operational reviews of regional- and market-level sales, pipeline, client prioritization, or operational issues.

The regional ABS lead is accountable for sales within the region. The role serves as a conduit between global and markets within the region and to coordinate resources across markets within the region. They are directly involved in supporting large sales in the region.

The market ABS lead is accountable for sales in the market. This role should not develop or change offerings, solution standards, or tooling unless part of a regional or global initiative.

Now you can look horizontally and start to build the forums that will foster the right conversations across job families at each layer. This is a quite different approach than the typical "job description" used for grade banding and pay decisions.

Figure 4.2 Real role description example

Global Product Leader

Role Overview

Create, drive, and align the vision and strategy for the product globally

Identify and develop offerings that will accelerate internal and external brand of the product

Build and maintain strategic product eco-system partnerships through facilitation of co-created client solutions

Promote a culture of focused entrepreneurship across the product group by ensuring clarity and understanding of the strategy

Develop a talent strategy to ensure a pipeline of skills and experience to fuel the product offering development

Actively support local leaders to originate and sell product solutions and drive major strategic pursuits

Collaboration Partners

The high trust relationships I need to build outside of my immediate team are:

- Technology Leadership Team members (names)
- Market Leads (names)
- Innovation Lead (name)
- Enterprise Functions Leads (names)
- Industry Sector Leads (names)
- Key Account Leads (names)

Measures of Success

The key metrics that will define success for the coming year are:

- Increase sales of product overall from $xxx to $xxx
- Define a product talent strategy within each market to address projected skill gaps
- Increase number of joint client engagements with product eco-system partners
- Launch three new offerings

How I Spend my Time

Current Clients	Business Development	Offering Development	Management of the Team	Coordinating with Peers	External Speaking
20%	20%	20%	20%	10%	10%

Key Takeaways

- The vertical organization is an essential component of design and should be based on a hierarchy of thought and focus, rather than a hierarchy based on titles and status.
- Each leadership layer (strategic, integrative, and operational) in the organization should have a different time horizon and make a unique set of decisions in order to not overlap with the work of the layer below.
- A well-designed vertical organization empowers individuals by creating external accountability (expectations for what a role must deliver) and motivating internal responsibility (discretionary effort).

References

Drotter, S (2011) *The Performance Pipeline: Getting the right performance at every level of leadership*, Jossey-Bass, San Francisco

Hobson, A (2004) *The Oxford Dictionary of Difficult Words*, Oxford University Press, Oxford

Kesler, G and Kates, A (2016) *Bridging Organization Design and Performance: Five ways to activate a global operating model*, John Wiley & Sons, Inc, New York

Romme, A G L (2019) Climbing up and down the hierarchy of accountability: Implications for organization design, *Journal of Organization Design*, 8 (20)

The Horizontal Organization 05

Vertical organization plays an important role in creating clarity of focus and accountability. But the new disruptive business models being embraced in the 2020s require the building of sophisticated capabilities that incorporate digital, commercial, innovation, and other muscles across functions, geographies, and businesses lines. To fully serve the customer, leaders must enable seamless collaboration across internal boundaries and into the broader ecosystem. This can only be accomplished through horizontal organization.

The horizontal organization is a path to both agility and scale. Agility requires the assembly of assets, regardless of where they are created or produced, to meet unique customer needs. Scale is achieved by bridging services, platforms, and processes across business units.

Well-designed horizontal organization not only allows but also encourages people to join cross-boundary teams and networks and to take responsibility for results that they cannot deliver on their own. In the spirit of volunteerism, the horizontal organization relies heavily on behavior to succeed. All the elements of design must come together to foster discretionary responsibility, not just impose accountability. Removing barriers to proactive collaboration is hard work. It is certainly more than standing up cross-functional teams. Our identities tend to be connected to our most proximate team—the product line we work on, our location, or our professional functional group. Collaboration at scale—across teams—must be designed into the organizational wiring of the company. We have a strong natural desire as humans for collaboration within our home team, but often need to be helped to collaborate across team boundaries.

While the importance of working across boundaries to execute complex growth strategies is not a new idea, it is still elusive. Even many new-economy, digital natives have not mastered the collaboration challenge beyond teams. In this chapter we will cover:

- the horizontal organization imperative
- becoming center-led
- formal networks
- making horizontal organization successful

The Horizontal Organization Imperative

There are three compelling reasons to master horizontal organization. The first is the power of connecting people to purpose, to create a climate where people opt into a shared agenda. The second is the increasing power of the customer in today's evolving business. The third is digital technology and the migration of work to intelligent platforms.

People and Purpose

While vertical organization is the source of accountability in the enterprise, horizontal organization is what motivates discretionary responsibility. As one of our clients put it, "When the ball comes to me, I am thinking of the assist, not just the goal." Purpose-driven organizations are increasingly at the center of today's strategies and business models. Many acquisitions falter because they are driven by a different purpose than the acquiring company. Red Hat, now a part of IBM, has a strong ethos around democratizing software. Will these renegades be able to maintain their sense of purpose and retain their open-source culture? Can the small innovation teams of the cell and gene therapy group within Novartis co-exist with the big-pharma dominant culture there? These organizational challenges have to be solved at the interfaces of highly differentiated skills and cultures.

Without horizontal organization, leaders must rely on compliance-based, rather than commitment-based, systems to drive performance. The scramble for digital and artificial intelligence know-how is not being won just with higher compensation packages. Tech employees choose to stay with Mailchimp in the Atlanta area because the company has built a culture focused on a mission: supporting small business to communicate with customers. The call to action is strong for employees, and they come and stay for that mission.

The Dutch Professor and researcher Georges Romme offers an insight to the social science behind the tower and the square (Romme, 2019). He argues that conventional hierarchy is a "ladder of authority," and while this ladder is necessary to create clear accountability, when encumbered by too many layers and rules it tends to demotivate self-organizing activity. The organization needs to complement the ladder of authority with the "responsibility ladder." This is a self-directed process in which people choose to embrace the purpose and objectives of the organization and create value. The simpler the ladder of authority, the more likely people are to self-organize ladders of responsibility. We believe that the horizontal organization creates the mechanism for these ladders to be built. The objective for the organization designer should be to nurture these parallel systems and to embrace the tensions. Vertical organization creates clarity and focus of accountability. Horizontal organization produces ownership.

Customer-Centricity

The second compelling reason for attention to horizontal organization is that today's growth strategies and business models are increasingly focused on customer solutions and experiences.

Customer-centric strategies require operating models that drive solutions: bundles of products, services, and experiences that produce an integrated, positive customer experience. Services firms, such as Accenture, must serve clients by pulling from a dizzying array of specialized skill sets, from business and talent strategy and interactive marketing, to AI, intelligent platform services, and business process outsourcing. There is no way to deliver an integrated solution from these disciplines without wiring together complex webs of inter-relationships across the enterprise and beyond into the broader technology-partner ecosystem.

A large healthcare company that is radically shifting its business model can serve as an example. Through a series of acquisitions, this company aspires to deliver integrated, outcome-oriented solutions across diverse products and services, including pharmacy, medical equipment, healthcare insurance, and care delivery clinics. The bundled solutions combine a value proposition centered on more affordable and effective healthcare outcomes, often for chronically ill patients. The goal is close, sticky relationships with healthcare providers, payers, and patients across a complex and shifting ecosystem.

Companies such as this must be agile enough to continue to offer standalone services to some customers, while offering an integrated bundle of services to others. The legacy businesses often remain the dominant source of profit in these business models for years. New capabilities and shared services must be created or scaled to support the integrated offering. Some of these shared platforms, such as data and analytics and care delivery clinics, are built to deliver healthcare solutions across varied customer sets. Others act in support of the offering, such as technology infrastructure groups or provider and patient help centers. Go-to-market teams that manage customer accounts must be realigned in the front-end of the organization model to work across platforms with the know-how, motivation, and mechanisms that will allow them to bring sophisticated solutions to their existing and new accounts.

Some customers become "frenemies" in customer-centric ecosystems. They are customers for some portions of the new offering, while directly competing with other products or services within the bundle. Firewalls must be erected to protect proprietary and customer data. The go-to-market teams that manage provider and payer accounts in integrated healthcare providers, for example, must not have access to intelligence that sits in the delivery platforms.

The problem to solve in these complex organizational models is largely focused on the simultaneous need for massive specialization and for reliable, replicable integration for customers. In our healthcare example, the horizontal, customer-facing capability must co-exist with vertical structures that are deeply specialized in fields of science, technology, and medicine, and which must remain separated to protect legal and competing commercial interests. These are contradictions that can only be resolved by the horizontal organization working in concert with the vertical.

The Promise of Technology

Technology is also driving the need for robust horizontal organizations. It brings both threats and opportunities to existing business models. Collaboration is one of the biggest challenges to successful digital transformation. One survey of 1,500 global senior executives revealed that 75 percent of companies are still struggling with cross-function collaboration. Engineering, R&D, marketing, and operations functions are competing against each other in digitization efforts (Stacy, Narsalay, and Sen, 2020). The result is duplication of digital efforts and limited impact on revenue and productivity. The study authors concluded that companies that have seen the greatest return on their investments in technology have successfully broken down these barriers. Only then can the true power of cloud-based platforms and data sharing be harnessed.

Intelligent platforms, artificial intelligence, and digital capabilities can produce value-adding connections across both closely and loosely related business portfolios. But investments in technology cannot be fully exploited without corresponding changes in organization structures, culture, and skillsets. Successful digital leaders see themselves as weavers of digital into all aspects of the business strategy and organization, rather than the builder of stand-alone digital functions. They see the shared platforms that sit in the back of the organization model and are used by multiple business units and functions as providing not only greater productivity, but access to more resources.

Companies with loosely related business portfolios, and even holding companies, are seeking greater degrees of horizontal integration across business units, largely driven by data and analytics. Ulrich and Yeung have studied the evolving nature of today's diverse holding companies in what they have characterized as market-oriented ecosystems (Ulrich and Yeung, 2020). This evolving model seeks greater synergies among the business units as well as external ecosystem partners. The hub-and-spoke model of the conventional holding company is giving way to a network of business platforms that support the business units even in such classic conglomerates as Berkshire Hathaway, Tata Group, and General Dynamics. The business units leverage the technologies, services, and capital resources and know-how that sit in the platforms.

Becoming Center-Led

The debate over the benefits of a centralized versus decentralized organization is no longer useful. Figure 5.1 illustrates two very different dynamics that are easily confused in a conversation about how power and authority are to be delegated into the organization: the need for integration versus the need for control.

Control refers to the perceived need to manage risk and is represented on the X axis. Control can manifest through policies, reporting structures, norms, and performance management and reward systems.

Integration is the degree to which we must have connectivity among the business units, the functions, and the markets. It is represented on the Y axis with a scale from local to global. Local and global here don't refer merely to geography but also the continuum from the close-to-the-customer operating unit to the enterprise-wide corporate perspective.

Figure 5.1 Center-led

	Low	Control	High
Global / Integration	**Center-Led** Single strategy, common process and tools, clear decision guard rails, empowered teams (freedom within a framework).		**Centralized** Policy, fiduciary controls, centralized reporting.
Local	**De-Centralized** Autonomous business units with little functional or central guidance and little synergy expected.		**High Control, Low Integration** Bureaucracy.

There are circumstances when work and decisions should be centralized or decentralized, of course, but these are often quite clear and a small list. Some work and decisions—risk management, brand standards, big investments—should be centralized at the corporate level. Other work and decisions are so local, such as translations and local promotions, that no value can be added from people sitting outside a given market and are best left fully decentralized.

However, in most multi-dimensional companies, there are many decisions that require speed and local responsiveness, but also benefit from being aligned with a common, global agenda. It is this work that spans boundaries—vertical and horizontal—and must be coordinated that creates the most organization tension. Designing the balance between the forces of autonomy and integration is critical to designing successful horizontal organizations. Getting the right balance starts with avoiding the either/or of the centralization versus decentralization polarity.

Center-led is a construct that challenges conventional thinking about the nature of operating governance. A center-led organization (in the upper left quadrant of the framework) does not mean the work or decisions sit at the global or the enterprise level. In fact, in a center-led organization with high-functioning horizontal ways of working, the work (product innovation, brand campaign development, talent development, tech development, etc.) moves to where the capability and the capacity lives in the organization, anywhere in the world. It is very much about empowering the operating layer. However, the work is performed for the greater good of the company.

It can be scaled for application to multiple markets or franchises with limited localization and customization. The work is done within boundaries set with the enterprise growth strategy in mind.

In the center-led organization the company can use its size to leverage very specialized resources and move management time and attention around the world onto the highest value problems and opportunities. This can only be achieved if there is an enterprise view on talent, budget, resources, and priorities. The goal is to gain high degrees of integration without unnecessary controls. Empowerment is not abdication. It is freedom in a framework.

The center-led organization is built on:

- a shared enterprise strategy and leadership alignment on priorities
- formal networks across organizational boundaries
- shared organizational platforms (centers of expertise, shared services, information technology)
- clear decision guardrails
- common management and business processes
- collaborative metrics and incentives
- leaders who believe in the value of collaboration

Many of our clients have embraced the philosophy of center-led. It has the potential to end the debate about centralization and decentralization. But it is not easily executed. A leader in one company underlined a common misperception when we did a check-in assessment six months into implementation: "Those people in global are trying to make the new organization too center-led." This logic is similar to arguing a woman is too pregnant. Center-led is not a puzzle of degree. It is a way of behaving guided by the design. It is the strategic and integrative layers of the organization focusing on the right work to empower the operating layer and move innovation, knowledge, and talent horizontally across these units. What this executive was expressing was an honest feeling that the global groups were talking center-led but behaving through centralized controls. He was telling us that all the design levers had not yet been properly adjusted to create the right system of behavior as intended for this business.

Activating a center-led organization is a design and learning process that often takes many months or even years to realize. And, the challenges of loosening controls and moving from a highly centralized model to center-led are different, but no less vexing than shifting from a fractured, decentralized model toward more integration. Regardless of the starting point, without a clear commitment to becoming center-led—empowered but integrated—and a clear path that fits the business context and strategy, working across boundaries will be a struggle.

Formal Networks

When Jay Galbraith (Galbraith, 2010) introduced the "reconfigurable organization," he conceptualized it as a multi-dimensional matrix that remained relatively stable, boosted with a set of dynamic cross-boundary teams that would be formed around major growth and innovation opportunities and disband once the task was accomplished. This concept of reconfigurable teams sitting on top of a two- or three-dimensional stable structure is still useful. But today we can go beyond teams; we can design dynamic global networks powered by technology that allow people to work in real time around the world with common tools and data.

When we use the term network, we must distinguish here between an informal, relationship-based network and a formal organization network. Informal networks are between individuals. While they are necessary for cross-boundary work, they are not sufficient. High-trust, interpersonal working relationships are the foundation of organizations. Trust is a motivator of discretionary effort. Trust and the social capital that comes from it is important glue that binds the organizational parts together. But organizations can't be run solely on relationships, good will, and favors.

Formal networks are an organization entity. They have a distinct role and contribution from the other components. But they are comprised of people who also sit in the vertical structure of the organization. For example, think of a solution company that bundles products and services together. The product line may be responsible for innovation around a component. The commercial team identifies customer needs and makes the deal. But a network that cuts across products and markets to create the replicable, profitable offerings is also needed. We don't want every commercial unit reinventing solutions or hunting around to discover whether someone else has solved the same problem in a different market.

What makes a network different than a matrix is that a network is a membership construct. The members of a formal network are not a unique set of people. In our example, they are already in the markets or product lines. The distinction is subtle, but important. A matrix is built on two or more organizational units that come together through dual reporting lines.

A formal network is woven into the fabric of the organization. When they are successfully designed, local and global interests are met through the normal course of management and business processes.

Therefore, formal networks have to be designed to make them an integral part of the business. Reward systems and metrics must make it rational—part of the everyday work—to collaborate and for senior leaders to invest the time to create the conditions for collaboration. Business and management processes have to align work, making it easier for teams to come together. People should be selected into these teams considering soft skills and behaviors. There must be decision-making forums built to manage trade-offs that serve the greater company interests. There may be network leadership, but these leaders should see themselves as integrators, rather than managers of a distinct organizational dimension.

Just like a matrix, however, the use of networks can quickly overload an organization with collaboration. It is not uncommon for people sitting at critical nodes to be members of three or more teams and find their calendar full of mandatory weekly meetings and all manner of discussions where they have little to offer. Just like a matrix, effective formal networks need leaders to be adept at the dance of leaning in and letting go. Being inclusive, but also trusting colleagues. Finding the right balance to minimize internal coordination takes practice, reflection, and adjustment to both management processes and individual behaviors. Effective organization networks can't be installed. They have to be designed and built over time.

When designing, it may be helpful to think about two types of formal networks. The first are capability networks that leverage scarce, valuable insights and assets and make them widely available across organizational units. The second are operational networks that provide a standing-governance forum for oversight of complex boundary-spanning work.

Capability Networks

Capability networks start with the assumption that people, systems, and work are best placed in the operating units (product groups, geographies, or functions), but that the enterprise will benefit from tying them together. One benefit is talent attraction. Networks create professional communities, learning opportunities, and career paths that the operating unit can't offer to specialists. Another benefit is innovation. A capability network creates the mechanism to link and amplify insights and experiments for further investment. A third benefit is alignment. The network creates the forums to engage a diverse set of leaders from the integrative layer around strategic issues and investments.

"Digital" is an example of a capability that many legacy-analog companies are still working on building. The path to becoming a fully digital organization often begins with a fractured set of experiments undertaken by different business units, regions, and functions. Eventually, executives discover that the investments in these diverse assets are expensive and are not scalable in their decentralized configuration. The reflex is to bring in a chief digital officer at the enterprise level who begins to direct and control activities and investments. But digital is not a function that can be neatly bounded with reporting lines. The move from decentralized to centralized often merely creates a new set of frustrations and costs.

The key to developing networks is to think center-led. Tie these digital domains together through an integrated digital strategy closely connected to the core work of the business, linked through a cross-boundary network of resources that are supported by the right management processes, metrics, and skill profiles. Capability building depends upon a well-designed center that plays an active linking role guiding the right blend of global and local decision-making around shared priorities (Kesler and Kates, 2016).

A consumer products company provides an illustration. Over the course of 10 years, this company had built four types of digital capability, each living in different parts of the organization, as shown in Figure 5.2:

1 Digital brand and consumer engagement: The company website was a powerful social media platform led by effective content and access to digital applications that attracted high levels of membership. Enterprise marketing owned the brand across all physical and digital touchpoints.

2 E-commerce: The company built a robust e-commerce sales channel largely housed in the North America commercial unit but extended globally over time. A single technology backbone accommodated regionally oriented web pages.

3 Digital product (applications): Global category teams built a range of industry-leading digital apps, including wearables that connected with other physical and digital products. While core brand messaging from the marketing function served as inspiration for these ideas, this content tended to become disconnected from the global category teams.

4 Digital technology: Like many businesses, the company separated business digital technology from the core IT organization based on the logic that it needed to be driven by a very different cadence, culture, and skillset.

Figure 5.2 Digital components in a consumer product company

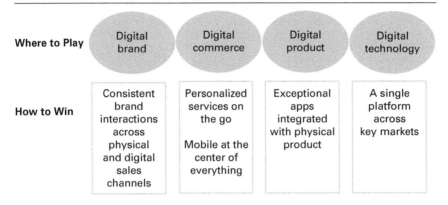

Where to Play	Digital brand	Digital commerce	Digital product	Digital technology
How to Win	Consistent brand interactions across physical and digital sales channels	Personalized services on the go Mobile at the center of everything	Exceptional apps integrated with physical product	A single platform across key markets

While each part of the business optimized its investment in digital activities, the lack of linkage across the work grew evermore obvious, especially when viewed through a user experience lens. A consumer spending time on the website who was taking in the substantial brand-oriented content might want to click through to purchase a product featured in the brand stories. This was not simple and intuitive, however, because the e-commerce pages were created by a different part of the organization. Likewise, innovative wearable and other digital apps created by the global category teams were not well represented in these brand content stories. Figure 5.3 shows how these activities were spread across the organization model.

Brand marketing, product creation, and commercial management, including company-owned as well as brick-and-mortar retail-partner stores, all had to become closely linked in order for the shopping experience to be seamless. But solving this was difficult, because while it was important to tie these distinct elements of digital business together (e-commerce, digital product, digital marketing, and the tech backbone) it was also necessary that each remain closely linked to its analog counterparts. If digital marketing was managed separately from the greater marketing team, the strategy would be diffused. If the e-commerce organization was separated from the core commercial organization channel conflicts would destroy value. If digital product teams did not remain closely tied to physical product, the apps might not function fully with the physical product. This conundrum cannot be solved with creating a new function or even dual reporting.

The company started by focusing on strategy. Leaders from across the organization were pulled together to build an integrated digital strategy for the enterprise. This customer-centered strategy identified the many touchpoints

Figure 5.3 Digital in the organization model

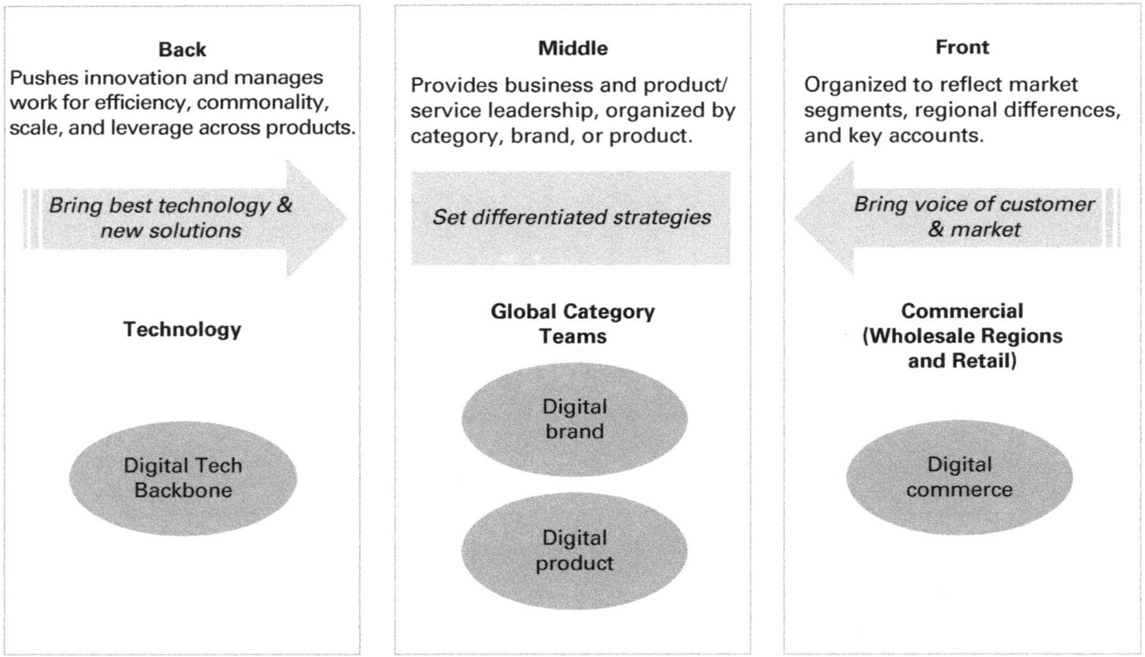

Back

Pushes innovation and manages work for efficiency, commonality, scale, and leverage across products.

Bring best technology & new solutions

Technology

Digital Tech Backbone

Middle

Provides business and product/service leadership, organized by category, brand, or product.

Set differentiated strategies

Global Category Teams

Digital brand

Digital product

Front

Organized to reflect market segments, regional differences, and key accounts.

Bring voice of customer & market

Commercial (Wholesale Regions and Retail)

Digital commerce

Figure 5.4 A network to link digital assets

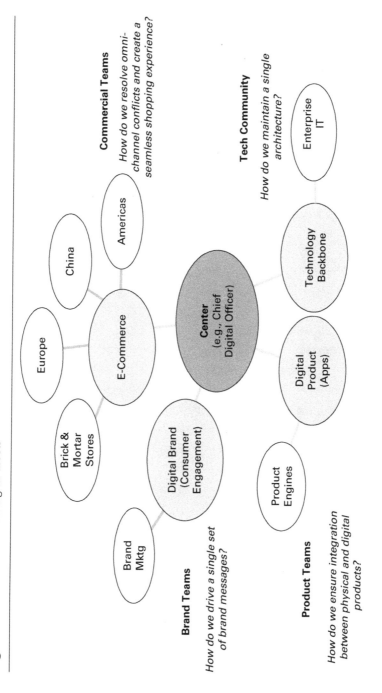

among the four key digital domains that were necessary to connect in order to create a single consumer experience.

The leaders who engaged in building the strategy became the basis of a standing forum, a digital community that was chartered to deliver the customer-centric strategy as shown in Figure 5.4. The gray figures represent domains in the larger digital community, while the white figures represent the core or legacy operating units of the business.

An organization design team worked to wire the formal network together with a thoughtful alignment of the points on the Star Model:

Structure: A new chief digital officer was brought in with accountability to drive the integrated digital strategy through to execution. The role reported directly to the CEO with a seat at the executive committee table to send a clear message about the power vested in the role. But the role was an integrator of talent and assets, not an owner. In order to balance the power given to this new role, reporting relationships for those in the digital network remained in the operating units that managed the business day-to-day. This was not a matrix with dual reporting.

Process: A meeting cadence was established for the digital network leadership, with standing agenda items heavily focused on integration and horizontal work. Decision rights were clearly articulated regarding specific technology- and application-development decisions as well as for investment funding within the digital domains.

Metrics: Business objectives were tightly aligned around the digital strategy, with shared ownership for key metrics such as web sessions, conversion rate, lifetime shopper value, and average order value.

The role of the center—in this example, represented by the chief digital officer—must be carefully designed in the formal network. Those in center-based leadership roles are tasked with driving a common agenda, aligning priorities, and coordinating a shared set of initiatives and capabilities. They are not directive, and they are not controlling. Success is based on community-building and how well these center roles inspire teams to work together to serve customers.

Operational Networks

Operational networks have a job to do beyond creating community, building capability, or aligning agendas. All these elements are part of their work, but they have an additional role. Operational networks create unique offerings that no one part of the core organization can create on its own. As with capability networks, the people live in their function or operating unit. But, they can be members of one or more networks, and that membership is a formal role, accountable to the network and the business priorities it serves. These outputs typically include building solutions across multiple software, product, and service components, or delivering components of an ecosystem that reaches beyond the company boundaries. Member participation in these operational networks can be fluid around a governing core of team members that will remain constant. Other network members may participate as the workload requires. But they may remain members, regardless of the current task.

Again, an example will help. Accenture is a global professional services firm of more than 500,000 people, serving clients in 120 countries, across more than 40 industries. In 2020, leadership shifted the operating model from a strong center of gravity focused on global, industry-aligned business units, to a largely regional market model in order to enable client-centric solutions. The company's wide array of services in strategy, consulting, interactive digital, technology, and operations had become too diverse to easily integrate. Clients were demanding deep industry and functional expertise combined with specialized support in a number of disciplines and practices, including intelligent platforms, artificial intelligence, business process outsourcing, business strategy, and consulting support. Empowered geographic-market units would enable integration of these many assets close to the clients, where configurable solutions can be tailored.

CEO Julie Sweet was determined that while the commercial focus of the company would shift into 20 front-line market units, this would not be a swing of the power pendulum from global to local. This new organization would balance strong, client-centric market units that would tailor solutions across the practices and disciplines, with a set of four heavy-duty global service organizations that would oversee the robust array of technology and business capabilities.

This left the question of where critical industry expertise should be embedded. Deep knowledge of consumer products, retail, media, and many other industries must be both local and global. Generalist financial services experience is not enough. Deep knowledge of retail banking in Japan is the level of granularity clients were expecting. But this knowledge also has to be connected globally in order to create offerings that incorporate Accenture's unique blend of assets and scale. And only through a global lens can industry convergence trends (such as healthcare and technology, or technology and automotive) be captured.

The solution to threading industry expertise through all of the practices and disciplines was industry networks. These are operational networks accountable for client insights, end-to-end positioning, and offering development. Solution components are powered by the services (technology, strategy, etc.), with extensive engagement at the market-unit level. But the industry networks must develop the bundled offerings for a given industry. This work is led from the center, aligned with enterprise priorities, but the market units, as members of the networks, are fully engaged in the process.

What is interesting about the Accenture approach is that there are very few roles that are exclusively industry specialized. Rather, most everyone based in a market has two additional roles—a service specialty (e.g., strategy) and an industry specialty. In this way the industry networks integrate the voice of the global services while remaining intimately tied to the work and interests of the market unit client groups.

The ability for formal networks to bridge greater spans of influence, inside the company and even across a wider external ecosystem, makes them both powerful and problematic. They are a compelling and elegant design solution when a capability or offering cannot be created effectively in any other way. As a practical matter, however, they require intensive leadership attention, sustained over time.

Making Horizontal Organization Successful

Our work helping companies bring center-led, formal networks to life in complex environments yields a number of observations regarding what leads to success.

1 Shared purpose

A network can only create shared purpose for priorities that are part of the business strategy. Members in networks usually have "day jobs" with their own set of objectives. But when the network is activated around the right idea, the members come together with shared interests. At VF's North Face apparel business unit, the brand is positioned the same in China as it is in Europe and North America. Team members share a vision. A new product idea can come from anywhere, and ideas in the network are quickly shared. Members of the network in any region have an opportunity to join in building a business case for a new product. If the idea gains traction across regions it becomes scalable, and these are the projects that will get priority funding. Members of the network will be more likely to opt in when the core design idea has forward-compatible characteristics, meaning local developers can build on the core to make the concept more relevant to local customers without duplicating investments.

2 Compelling leadership
The role of leaders in horizontal networks is very different from those who run self-contained operating units. Networks are powerful development experiences for future general managers and senior executives. (We will discuss this more in Chapter 8.) The essential talents and skills required to muster results without well-defined authority levels include creating a compelling vision that ties membership to a greater purpose. These leaders enjoy building community, engaging diverse perspectives, and watching others get credit for great outcomes. Variations in leadership effectiveness have a direct impact on the effectiveness of networks.

Leaders need to be supported to work successfully in the horizontal organization, especially if they have been promoted and rewarded largely based on leading their own units. Many leaders don't see the value or don't know how to lead without formal authority and reporting lines. Especially when power dynamics are not clearly spelled out and leaders are left to figure it out on their own, the rational response is to resort to old habits that worked in the past.

Therefore, at the key nodes where value is going to be created, leaders and their teams need to be empowered and enabled to make decisions together, so they are motivated to take responsibility for a good enterprise outcome. Underneath the mechanics is an organizational investment in trust-building across boundaries, modeled by senior leaders.

3 Operating mechanisms
When networks are an important element in delivering business results, they must have clear presence in the company's operating model. They will be measured on core business results, along with vertical business units and functions. But they are also well served with metrics that reflect the unique, horizontal contribution they make to the business, tied directly to the uptake and consumption of solutions. In addition, decision rights and decision-making forums should be designed for within the network as well as the connection of the network to other business and management processes.

4 Activation

Design of the horizontal organization is not a one-and-done activity. The horizontal organization is in tension with the vertical organization. Often leaders are sitting in both constructs, sometimes wearing multiple hats in the same meeting. Each organization requires the right balance of these tensions. And, each organization has a different journey depending upon the starting culture and norms. Becoming center-led and building effective formal networks requires learning. Each cycle of decision-making has to be reflected upon. What worked and what needs to be adjusted? Are we seeing friction because of poorly designed or run management forums or decision rights? Do we not have the right leader profiles in place and clear behavioral expectations? Do our metrics and performance processes make these behaviors easy? Continuous assessment and adjustment are at the foundation of successful horizontal organization.

Key Takeaways

- Well-designed horizontal organization is important as a way to create shared purpose, organization across boundaries for customers, and to truly gain the power of investment in technology and new business models.

- Center-led avoids the false choice of centralized and decentralized, and the confusion between control and integration. It provides the benefits of scale and coordination of effort that can only be accomplished by the center and the benefits of empowered, local teams able to move quickly, but working within a shared strategy.

- Formal networks are an organization entity with a distinct role and contribution. But they are comprised of people who also sit in the vertical structure of the organization. This dual membership, with an agenda orchestrated by the center, allows the organization to quickly reconfigure to innovate and deliver work while leveraging assets across the company.

References

Galbraith, J R (2010) The multi-dimensional and reconfigurable organization, *Organizational Dynamics*, 1 (2), 115–25

Kesler, G and Kates, A (2016) *Bridging Organization Design and Performance: Five ways to activate a global operating model*, John Wiley & Sons, Inc, New York

Prahalad, C K and Oosterveld, J P (1999) Transforming internal governance: The challenge for multinationals, *MIT Sloan Management Review*

Romme, A G L (2019) Climbing up and down the hierarchy of accountability: Implications for organization design, *Journal of Organization Design*, 8 (20)

Rossman, J (2019) *Think Like Amazon: 50½ ideas to become a digital leader*, McGrawHill Education, New York

Stacy, N, Narsalay, R and Sen, A (2020) Together makes better: How to drive cross-function collaboration. https://www.accenture.com/us-en/insights/industry-x-0/cross-functional-collaboration (archived at https://perma.cc/495R-G9YQ)

Function Design 06

The functions in an organization are the mortar that holds the building blocks of a complex organization together. They are the source of foundational capabilities that help businesses compete, innovate, and deliver complex solutions to customers.

The HR function builds talent pathways across businesses by managing common approaches to selecting people, creating alignment with the right reward systems, and stewarding leadership talent as company-wide resources that can be readily moved across operating units and functions.

Procurement leverages buying power and relationships across the ecosystem to reduce costs and maintain quality.

Finance integrates a divisional structure by driving common measurement systems, setting financial targets, and helping to assure capital moves to the right opportunities across the portfolio.

Marketing ensures that the brand story is told consistently, and brand standards are lived up to even as geographic units adapt and localize product features, packaging, and delivery systems.

Corporate technology and supply chain organizations play similar critical roles in connecting and leveraging systems and processes.

Even in a loosely related portfolio of businesses, functions can ensure diverse enterprise assets are brought to bear in solving customer problems. Today, the demand for companies to be innovative, efficient, and locally responsive all at the same time makes the integrative and capability-building roles that functions play even more important.

Yet, in too many organizations, these functions are not seen as capability builders and integrators. They are seen as costly overhead, full of people that slow decisions and add complexity for the operating units. Even after decades of "transformation" projects in HR, finance, and other functions, progress remains elusive, and the frustration for operating unit executives as well as functional leadership incumbents remains high. Our assessment work with large, multinational companies reveals common themes across industries:

- Role confusion between the center-based functions and the businesses and regions. There is no real end-to-end view of the work resulting in duplication and uncoordinated programs.

- Poor hand-offs between centers of expertise that sit in "corporate" and their functional partners who sit in the business units. The result is overlap of effort, inconsistent execution, and weak delivery of critical know-how and practices. New product launches, talent management, data analytics and insights, and key technologies are slowed rather than enhanced.

- Failure to fully realize the shift of roles from risk management to strategic partner. Business leaders create their own shadow groups to get the responsive resources they feel they need and can control.

- Lack of alignment with line leaders on expectations and role manifested by complex projects rolled out from the center that aren't designed from a user experience perspective.

- Lack of visibility into the total cost of the function, fractured budget ownership, and arbitrary inconsistencies in resource levels from business to business.

Many of the companies that we have mentioned in this book have redesigned their functions to drive integration across businesses "end-to-end." This means examining all activity and resources in the center, across geographies, and into the business units as a single value stream. The work is realigned and placed in the optimal parts of the organization. They utilize technology to drive productivity in the way internal partners and customers are served. And, they have aligned the functions to avoid unnecessary duplication of infrastructure up and down through the layers of the organization.

We have found three frameworks and sets of practices critical to designing enterprise functions in a systemic, aligned manner. These frameworks can make the difference between reshuffling roles and bringing real change to the value that functional infrastructure brings the enterprise:

1 Service delivery model: How we serve internal customers.

2 Function value work definition: How we group and place work in the organization, end-to-end.

3 Functional architecture blueprint: How functional units are layered in the operating model of the company.

Figure 6.1 Service delivery model for HR

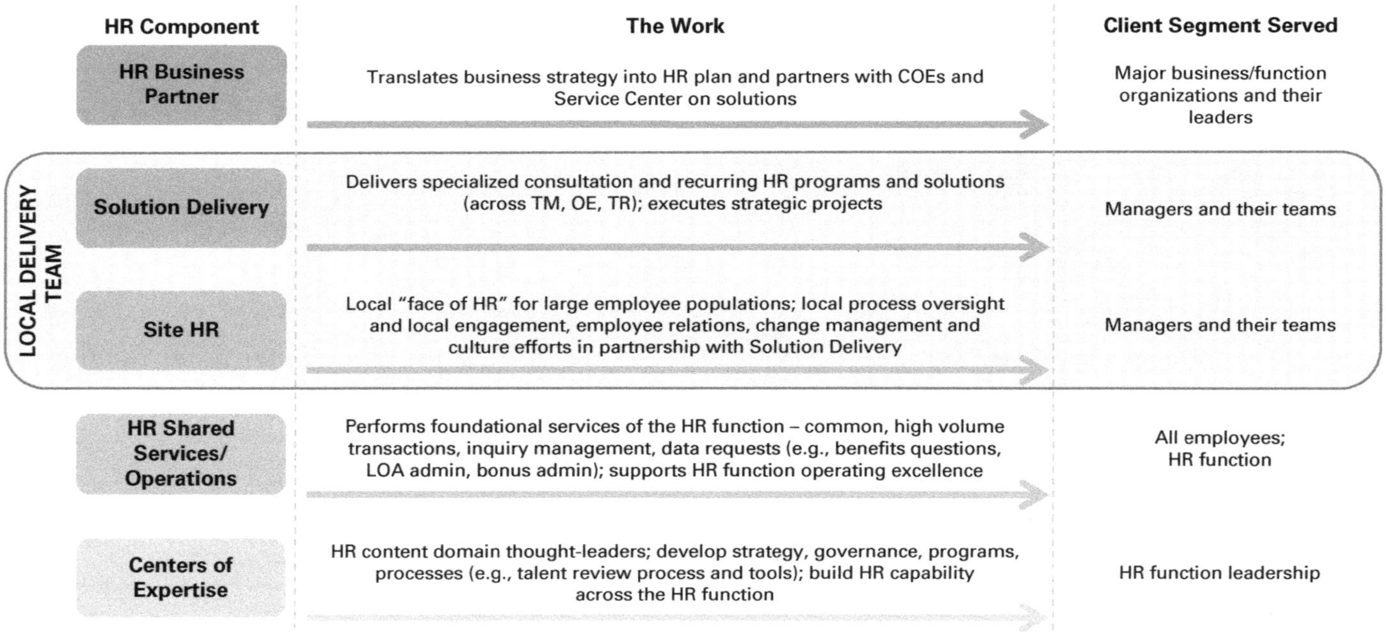

HR Component	The Work	Client Segment Served
HR Business Partner	Translates business strategy into HR plan and partners with COEs and Service Center on solutions	Major business/function organizations and their leaders
Solution Delivery	Delivers specialized consultation and recurring HR programs and solutions (across TM, OE, TR); executes strategic projects	Managers and their teams
Site HR	Local "face of HR" for large employee populations; local process oversight and local engagement, employee relations, change management and culture efforts in partnership with Solution Delivery	Managers and their teams
HR Shared Services/ Operations	Performs foundational services of the HR function – common, high volume transactions, inquiry management, data requests (e.g., benefits questions, LOA admin, bonus admin); supports HR function operating excellence	All employees; HR function
Centers of Expertise	HR content domain thought-leaders; develop strategy, governance, programs, processes (e.g., talent review process and tools); build HR capability across the HR function	HR function leadership

LOCAL DELIVERY TEAM

The Service Delivery Model

Too often, we have seen functional leadership teams spend countless hours on a strategy only to come up with a generic statement that could be used by almost any other organization. Function strategy is simple—it is to support execution of the business strategy. For example, if the company strategy is to grow through acquisition, then both HR and finance should be sure they are focused on building capabilities around due diligence and integration.

We find that a clear set of priorities and a well thought through service delivery model is more useful than a functional strategy. The service delivery model helps a leadership team make hard choices about the best way to align scarce resources against internal client segments. It helps answer where staff will be deployed and where automation and other productivity enablers will be applied. Figure 6.1 shows an example for an HR function.

In this example, it is now clear what we expect of the "HR business partner" role, which is often poorly defined and staffed without clarifying how and where the role adds the most value. The role is clearly focused on supporting leadership of the major business units and functions, while all transactional services are automated in a shared services unit.

These models are best viewed as the opening conversation in the design process. They need not be complex. The goal is to start with key stakeholder groups and to consider the points of interaction and critical value-adding outputs to be delivered to each.

The model may change over time and can be treated as something of a work in progress, but to land a point of view about who are the key constituents, partners, or customers, and how they will be served, is an excellent starting discussion.

The Function Value Framework

After getting alignment on a top-down view of what services will be delivered and through which part of the function, the next step is to look at how the grouping and delivery of work might change. The important work of the function for today and tomorrow is identified and sorted into a value framework that provides the granularity to make hard choices about what work is a priority and where it should be placed in the organization. There are four categories of functional work that are relevant to nearly all functional organizations:

- function oversight and compliance
- centers of expertise (thought leadership)
- shared services (professional and transactional)
- business-unit embedded support (business partner)

All retained functional work should fit into one of the four buckets and should meet the "rules" that accompany that work. Work that does not fit into the rationale for each category is a candidate for elimination. Figure 6.2 shows the function value framework.

Function Oversight and Compliance

This is the work of the top functional executive team. It is policy work and, where necessary, requires a level of authority to achieve compliance. Functions should be expected to create solutions that address the vexing problems the business has charged them to solve. In finance, that means how the company will manage debt and equity, how to manage currency fluctuations, and how to assure fiduciary compliance. In human resources, it means how to source and reward the right talent, how to shape culture, how to develop future leaders, and how to manage employment law risks. The outputs should be few but robust, linked to the business model of the company, and appropriate to its size and geographic complexity. The "rule" here is straightforward: policy, fiduciary requirements and high-level strategy are treated as "mandatory."

Centers of Expertise

The nature of this work is often the most difficult to define effectively and tends to expand in scope. These are the thought leaders and program designers, the specialists that bigger organizations can afford. The pay-off of scale. The key to a well-designed center of expertise is to be very selective about subject matter focus and then to staff with high-powered players who will bring the best ideas to the business. This is the work of the "few and the fabulous," argues one of our CHRO clients. These are not service-delivery people; they should be too few in numbers to get involved deeply in hands-on initiatives. They build capabilities, tools, and practices that their colleagues

Figure 6.2 Function value framework

	Center-Led (Needed by All or Most)				Embedded in Operating Units
	Functional Oversight	**Thought Leadership**	**Transaction Shared Services (Contact Center/Back Office)**	**Professional Shared Services (Solutions Delivery)**	**Business Partner**
Client	"Brand standards and risk management"	"Deep content expertise and thought leadership for the enterprise"	"High volume, predictable transactions and data management"	"Specialized client support close to the business"	"Strategic, function/business-specific diagnostics and solutions"
	Enterprise	Functional business partners, leaders, functional colleagues	All employees	Managers and their teams	Executive function/operating unit leaders and their teams
Key Activities	■ Functional strategy and policy, worldwide ■ Global standards, identification and stewardship of key capabilities ■ Fiduciary controls, compliance	■ Thought leadership; deep expertise ■ Best practices and measurement ■ Capability development across enterprise ■ Expert consultants—accelerate getting the work done	■ Activities tangential to the core work of the business units ■ Pooled for scale and efficiency ■ Highly repetitive, transactional work activities	■ Execute core programs and processes and work with business partners to solve complex problems ■ Inform the design and development of new programs and processes ■ Work across functions/lines of business	■ Business strategy development ■ Consultation and business unit decision making support ■ Provide insights back to the center
Rationale	■ Basis of global strategy and approach to growth ■ High-value investments ■ Risk management	■ Expertise that is difficult or expensive to replicate ■ Best ideas attract users ■ Design once for everyone	■ Selective basis only: • Substantial economies available • Commonality desirable ■ Best alternative: central, field-based, outsourced	■ Execution of projects and processes that require experienced talent with specialized skills and local knowledge, using standard methods and tools	■ Assured execution of business imperatives ■ Embedded with business but often with reporting line back to function leader in the center
Value	Enterprise brand and risk management	Decision support	Speed and service	Specialist delivery	Partnership
Rule	*Mandatory*	*Compelling ideas win*	*Mandatory once agreed to by operating units*	*Use common tools and processes where possible*	*Close to the business, but don't invent new tools*

Shared Services (spanning Transaction Shared Services and Professional Shared Services) and the business need to execute shared strategies. At the corporate level these must be capabilities that fit most or all the businesses in the portfolio.

The deliverables of the thought leaders are leverageable programs, best practices, new processes, expert consulting and training of others. They provide critical knowhow and insights to policy makers. The rule here is that "the most compelling ideas win." Business units may refuse these deliverables, but the key is to make the ideas so compelling that internal customers seek them out because they are the best solutions available to solve this company's business problems. These teams should start small and build on quick wins with sustained focus over time.

Centers of expertise are most effective in closely and loosely related portfolios. They sit outside the operating unit, providing resources that the individual units could not afford on their own. And they serve to integrate by moving ideas and best practices across boundaries. In the closely related portfolio, most units will use the center of excellence. In a more loosely related portfolio, the units can more freely opt in and out, choosing whether programs or services are useful to them. These thought leadership functions are most difficult to find reason to establish in holding companies, where interests are diffused, and the operating governance is more of a confederation.

Shared Services

Shared services organizations have made their way into most companies as the opportunities to consolidate, automate, outsource, and move to low-cost labor locations have become available. The conversation here is: do we build, buy, borrow, or bot?

Real gains can be realized by integrating service teams in logical geographic clusters who then service multiple business units, supported by technology. These organizations need solid business cases, reviewed in detail and endorsed by the business leaders, with payoffs and service standards that can be measured. Service contracts must be laid out in detail, committing the service delivery units to specific service targets such as cycle time, throughput, and cost per transaction.

Once there is a clear, contracted understanding around the value framework, the options for service delivery and organization structure are numerous. At The Coca-Cola Company, the HR chief challenged design teams to avoid centralizing thought-leadership work in the Atlanta headquarters.

Instead, teams completed an exhaustive inventory of internal best practices. They discovered, for example, that Europe ran the best general-management education programs, Latin America had seated the best practice for performance management, and so on.

Many companies are moving beyond traditional shared services of call centers and transaction processing. In fact, much of that work is being automated. The next wave of shared services are professional services teams for "solution delivery" work that requires a high level of expertise and close connection to a business or geography. Rather than just leveraging cost, efficiency, and consistency, these teams are leveraging knowledge and expertise. The key to these professional shared services is that they may be co-located in the business units or geographies, but they are managed by the center. They localize and adapt enterprise programs but don't invent new tools. For example, Nike activates its enterprise talent management practices through solution-delivery roles that report to the center but are sitting in the business units and major locations. These talent experts use the programs and tools developed by the center of expertise but apply local knowledge and relationships to directly inform and influence talent-planning outcomes that are relevant to the business.

The rule here is "mandatory participation once the businesses have signed on" to the business case. If the businesses can opt out of enterprise shared services and build their own, the cost structure is impacted, and the employee experience is inconsistent. But, since one size rarely fits all, the service contract must be designed with all parties involved.

Business-Unit Embedded Support

It is here that the "business partners" draw from the center-led resources defined above to create and deliver solutions to their client business units. These players should be strong on diagnostics and assembling solutions. They can be advocates for the unique needs of the business unit, market, or audience they support. But, they do so without inventing new tools, processes, or practices. Their mantra should be to adapt, adopt, and deliver.

Functional Architecture Blueprint

Once the service delivery model is clear and the work has been identified in the function value framework, a critical task remains before drawing organizational charts. The functional architecture blueprint looks end-to-end at the work of the function and maps it to the business. In this way work, decisions, and decision support are placed at the right layers in the vertical structure. When this is done with a view across functions, it is even more powerful. Although each function is designed fit for purpose, the service delivery model and the function value framework provide a consistent logic. A general manager will have a set of business partners around the table all providing insightful decision support. Or, shared service hubs can be combined and managed together at a low-cost location in a region. An example is shown in Figure 6.3. This simple illustration draws immediate debate among functional and business leaders, and it is a debate well worth having.

In this example, shared services are placed in the regions due to the extensive operations around the globe. Lean teams of business partners are placed in the business segments and countries, as this is the anchor layer for the company, the operating center of gravity. Centers of expertise sit exclusively in the corporate layer due to this company's intent to move to a much more integrated and cost-efficient operating model.

When developing the blueprint, it is important to go back to the operating framework of the company to determine how integrated the overall enterprise is expected to be, and how much synergy is required across business units and geographies. For example, in the more integrated operating model, we would expect more centers of expertise to sit at the corporate layer with little or no duplication of expertise in the business units (think McDonald's). In the loosely related business model—especially where businesses share few or no customers, technologies, or cost synergies—we would expect functions to be based more within these diverse businesses with a very thin, compliance-oriented corporate layer (think United Technologies).

Even an "as-is" version of the illustration can be a surprising, if not jolting, discovery that helps to facilitate a healthy conversation about how to realign the architecture in the future state. The power of the blueprint is that it helps avoid duplication and over-layering of common work, a major cause of unrewarded organization complexity.

Figure 6.3 Function architecture blueprint

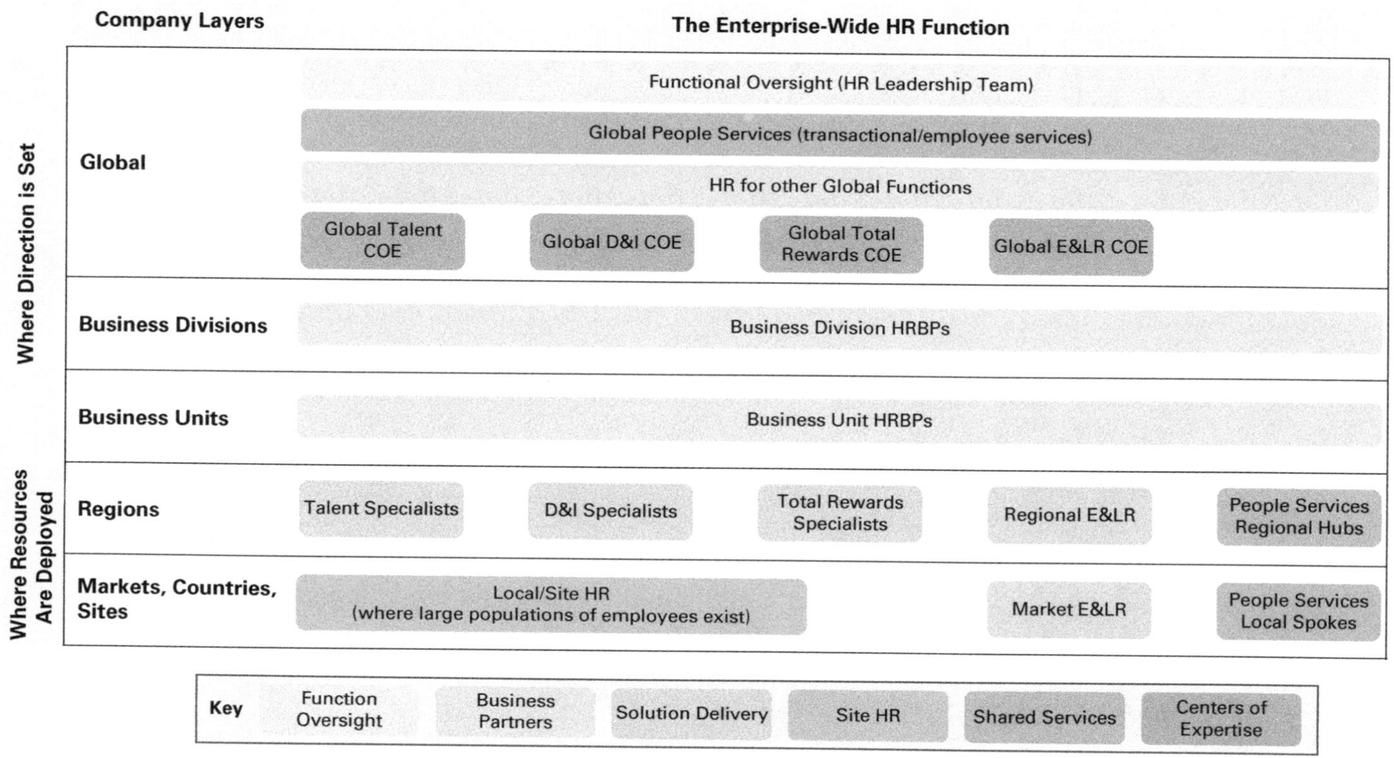

The Enterprise-Wide HR Function

Company Layers

Company Layers				
Global	Functional Oversight (HR Leadership Team)			
	Global People Services (transactional/employee services)			
	HR for other Global Functions			
	Global Talent COE	Global D&I COE	Global Total Rewards COE	Global E&LR COE
Business Divisions	Business Division HRBPs			
Business Units	Business Unit HRBPs			
Regions	Talent Specialists	D&I Specialists	Total Rewards Specialists	Regional E&LR	People Services Regional Hubs
Markets, Countries, Sites	Local/Site HR (where large populations of employees exist)		Market E&LR	People Services Local Spokes

Where Direction is Set

Where Resources Are Deployed

Key | Function Oversight | Business Partners | Solution Delivery | Site HR | Shared Services | Centers of Expertise

Key Takeaways

- The realignment of enterprise functions to deliver greater value to the growth agenda is a critical part of rethinking the operating model of a company.

- Function leaders should start with a service delivery model that identifies audiences and stakeholders and what essential work needs to be delivered to each.

- The future work of the function should be identified in a granular way, sorting activities into the function value framework (compliance, centers of expertise, shared services, and business unit embedded).

- The overall architecture of the function should be mapped against the company's operating organizational layers and units into a blueprint. Then and only then does it make sense to prepare organizational charts that show reporting relationships.

- The blueprint is most powerful when all functions are viewed side by side to assure a coherent logic for the overall infrastructure of the company.

- When all functions are designed around the same frameworks, there is a productive consistency and linkage to the company's overall operating model. The result is better execution of functional strategies, ultimately leading to higher functional contribution to the business at a lower overall cost.

Metrics

07

Metrics, and the accompanying incentives anchored to them, are among the most powerful drivers of behavior that organization designers can influence. "If strategy is the blueprint for building an organization, metrics are the concrete, wood, drywall, and bricks" (Harris and Tayler, 2019). Yet they may be the most likely to be overlooked in the design process. We call metrics and rewards the orphan point on the Star Model, a design element that many organization design initiatives avoid, postpone, or carelessly muddle through (Schuster and Kesler, 2011). The reasons are many, but at the core, metrics remain something of a technical chore. They are passed off to finance and compensation experts to figure out. Few leaders have the confidence or guidance to make them both measurable *and* strategically focused—especially when the strategy is complex and abstract. And fewer take the time to go beyond financial commitments to reason through how to wire human behavior to a given strategic outcome. However, we would suggest that designing metrics is a core leadership task and has to be owned at the top.

When metrics and rewards are not aligned with strategy, structures, roles, and business processes, the unintended consequences are many. It is tempting to blame cash incentives for the Wells Fargo debacle in which salespeople opened fake bank accounts for clients on a grand scale. But the metrics drove many motivators, including what some insiders described as relentless pressure to meet cross-selling targets. Strangely enough, cross-selling was not part of Wells Fargo's strategy at all. The metrics took on a life of their own. Customers, and ultimately shareholders, suffered the consequences.

In organizations that need to be powered by cross-boundary capabilities, metrics play a critical role in wiring the elements together. To be sure, the virtual links that networks enable require effective processes. But without meaningful accountabilities, members of these abstract arrangements lose interest and are easily distracted from the hard work of getting things done across functions, borders, and lines of business.

Here are some of the value-destroying effects of poorly aligned metrics:

- Individual performance targets compete with the goals of business strategy.
- Rational decisions are made to optimize performance in one unit, contrary to the needs of the overall organization.

- Customers are denied the value and the seamless experience that the collective capabilities of the organization can bring to bear.

- Roles and accountabilities are confused, which creates friction and destroys trust.

- The organization is slow to act and burdened with internal conflicts.

- Leaders resist change (because it is rational to do so when incentives encourage old behaviors).

Conversely, well-designed metrics, rewards, accountabilities, and roles create a system that becomes the "software" that runs the operating model of a company. This system makes clear what success looks like at the individual and team level, motivates collaboration and innovation, and incentivizes the leadership behaviors that are critical to the strategy.

An Organizational View of Accountabilities

Accountability is the basis for defining metrics, and ultimately, rewards systems. When accountabilities are part of the design of the organizational system, metrics will be more easily aligned with business objectives. Let's start with the operating model, and consider what a given set of choices means for accountability (Table 7.1).

These accountability questions are actually design questions. They highlight the iterative nature of the design process. As we answer them, we are giving depth to the operating model, which naturally leads to role definition, process definition, and rewards-system decisions. In this way, the development of metrics is not an afterthought or something that happens later in the design process, but it is an integral part of the core design work.

Defining accountabilities helps the leadership team choose the best primary grouping logic (function, product, geography, or customer). A creative way to puzzle through the pros and cons of each option is to ask the questions: What lens do you want your leaders looking through as they make decisions? What data should inform their work and how they track progress? In the Gillette razor business, the focus is brand, not product. Brand metrics drive brand leaders to embrace cannibalization and planned obsolescence of older models in order to continue innovation into newer shaving systems with a higher value proposition and price points for blades. Roles and metrics aligned by product might lead to different strategies aimed at preserving current products or focusing energy inward on cost reduction and profit margins.

Table 7.1 Operating model and accountabilities

Operating Model Choices	Accountability Questions
What relationship among assets in the business portfolio will deliver the most value to customers?	• What are the customer touch points in the new organization? • What roles are accountable for customer performance? • How will we measure customer value?
What is the basic shape of the organization model?	• How do we measure roles that sit in the "front" of the model? • How do we measure roles that sit in the "middle" of the model? • How do we measure roles that sit in the "back" of the model?
What capabilities are owned at the enterprise level, creating integration across the businesses, and which are owned at the business unit level?	• Who owns critical capabilities at the enterprise and the operating unit levels? • How much risk-taking should leaders take in the innovation process? • How will we measure the effectiveness of key capabilities?
Where should accountability for business results be placed in the organization?	• Which roles will be accountable for the growth strategy? • What roles are accountable for profit and loss? • How far down in the hierarchy should profit and loss be delegated (to avoid sub-optimizing results)?

(continued)

Table 7.1 (Continued)

Operating Model Choices	Accountability Questions
What are the roles of business units, functions (operating and enabling), and markets?	• How do decision rights need to be aligned with accountabilities? • What are the right measurement entities in the organization, and at what level?
What is the right balance of power across those components?	• Which roles need to share or manage complementary metrics to assure collaboration? • At what level of the organization should "team results" (for a common agenda) be measured? • What behaviors will be critical in executing our plans?
Where do we need integration and where do we want separation across lines of business?	• What is the weighting of team vs. individual results that needs to be built into the performance management system? • How do we measure separate units that must work outside the core profit engine of the company?
What is the ecosystem within which this business operates, and what connections need to be made?	• What is the nature of partnerships outside the corporation? • Which metrics should be shared among ecosystem partners? • How do we protect the interests of individual members in the system?

A quick example illustrates the iterative nature of design choices and accountabilities. Consider the placement of sales results in a company with multiple product divisions. When accountability for sales is placed in the product division instead of a regional market, the result is a self-contained business unit. The product division general managers like this design because they have control. They can make product decisions that drive sales. This design choice simplifies decision-making by establishing a single point of accountability for total business results. But that choice comes with trade-offs.

If each business unit manages its own sales organization, it will incur more cost due to duplicated resources. If we have a closely related portfolio of businesses, opportunities for leveraging investment in common systems, training, and sales operations may be missed. No matter how well each division general manager runs their unit there is a cost and this decision, which is one of both organizational architecture and metrics, places the cost of these duplicated resources on the enterprise.

Conversely, if the company has a loosely related portfolio and the businesses do not share common customers or go-to-market approaches, investment in common systems, training, and sales operations creates a different cost. Here we may have corporate staff people creating policies and practices that do not meet any customer-relevant needs of the business and the cost will be borne by the business units. The metrics of our general managers and our functions must align with the operating model.

Vertical Alignment

In Chapter 4 we argued the importance of designing layers in the organization to assure unique, valued-adding leadership work at each level. This clarity of the essential role of leadership layers is key to vertical alignment of accountabilities. We introduced three core layers in the vertical organization, as shown in Figure 7.1.

We recommend a sequence in the way companies lay out the vertical view of accountabilities up and down through the three layers:

1 Start with the *operating* unit layer (the anchor layer for front-line execution).

2 Then, determine accountabilities for the *strategic* layer (creators of the growth strategy and common agenda).

3 Finally, align the *integrative* layer (connectors across boundaries and builders of common process and culture).

Figure 7.1 Layers of leadership work

Strategic Leadership Layer
- Vision, portfolio management, priorities
- Big bet and trade-off decisions
- Single voice for purpose and culture
- Accountable for big bets

Integrative Leadership Layer
- Translating strategy into execution
- Linkage forums, systems, processes
- Structuring connections across boundaries

Anchor Business Layer (Operating Layer)
- Serving customers profitably
- Execution of shared strategies
- Front-line ownership of business results
- Ears on the ground—intelligence capture

We start with the operating unit layer—the front line for execution of the business plan—as this is the anchor layer that must deliver the results for the enterprise. Decisions in the operating layer typically include customer prioritization and coverage, service execution, sales management through delivery, tactical pricing, and managing advertising and promotion activity. In companies that deliver complex customer solutions, these are the leaders who will bundle the components to meet customer needs. The metrics for this layer are the core measures of the business. The components of the P&L and all of the measures of customer performance will be owned here. Metrics for the operating unit layer may include:

- revenue growth
- profit contribution
- customer service
- cost of selling
- product/service mix
- new product launch effectiveness

The more closely related the portfolio (column 2 in the operating framework), the higher up in the organization the P&L should sit to avoid suboptimization. In this way, you drive shared success. When the P&L sits high up then a set of metrics are developed for each part of the business that matches their contribution to the overall outcome. Together, these metrics make up the full P&L.

Next, it is useful to focus on the strategic leadership layer. This layer creates the common agenda, including the growth strategy, investment allocation, and critical initiatives. As a practical matter, this layer may include the top executive team in the organization as well as the global units that oversee the growth strategies and manage global offerings for the lines of business. Setting the metrics for the strategic layer, which represents the worldwide interests of the global company, can be challenging. There is nearly always a tension between the need for accountability (ensuring that global teams are "on the hook" for results) and the need to be certain that these strategy layer roles are not attempting to micro-manage results that are rightly the primary accountability of the operating unit layer.

The accountabilities of the strategic layer could include:

- effectiveness of the strategic plan
- new product pipeline
- brand strength
- market share and uptake of global offerings (products and services)
- marketing program effectiveness
- product/service profitable growth, worldwide
- global ecosystem strategy and relationships
- quality of strategic initiatives

Care must be taken in aligning vertical accountabilities to avoid the temptation to create metrics that will cause strategic leadership to spend time tracking quarterly results in each market, pressuring the operating units to respond to gaps, or demanding data and special reporting from the markets. It is useful to identify what the strategic layer of leadership will *not do*. Examples of the wrong behaviors include operational review of sales, customer pipeline and prioritization, and staffing decisions. Instead, the behaviors we want from the strategic layer might include understanding broad trends in uptake of new products (and corrective action plans), analyzing broad trends in profitability (with planned adjustments in cost of goods sold), and measuring and driving marketing and other key capabilities.

The integrative layer is often the most difficult to measure and to hold accountable for concrete results. Leaders at this level are neither developers of strategy, products and services, nor are they the front-line operating unit. The integrative leadership layer often manages a portfolio of businesses or commercial regions, and these leaders must avoid the temptation to behave as though they are executing the plan. They will translate the global strategy for regional relevance, and they will make decisions about resource balancing across the portfolio. Naturally, they will be accountable for the cumulative results of their portfolio, but they must do so in a manner that serves the greater good of the company, avoiding decisions that facilitate achieving the overall revenue target at the expense of achieving the goals for a new product or service offering that may be more difficult.

Consider the risks in setting the wrong metrics for roles in the integrative layer:

- Incumbents may be motivated to work at the operating level, interfering with or micromanaging those who should be accountable for results.
- Overlapping responsibilities lead to slow decision-making, unrewarded complexity, and cost.
- Incumbents under-value and under-invest in work with peers including innovation acceleration, leader development, and building capabilities.

The challenge of this middle layer is to find unique ways to add value. The accountabilities of leaders in the integrative layer might include:

- profitable growth across a portfolio of markets or lines of business
- talent development, retention, and employment brand
- market development (commercial strategies, market access, integrated channel development, etc.)
- new product launch effectiveness
- regional customer outcomes (service levels, bigger and more valuable sales, customer satisfaction)
- strategic initiative implementation, bridging operating units
- selling, general and administrative (SG&A) cost management

Horizontal Alignment

A good place to start the conversation about horizontal alignment of metrics is with the customer, as discussed in Chapter 5. Customer value can and should be measured. Vanguard, the investment powerhouse, is an example of a very large enterprise that has built and maintained a reputation for creating customer value. Vanguard and others like it place as much energy in tracking customer value as they do in tracking other key assets. Metrics of customer value include revenue per new customer, purchases per customer, and increasingly, net promoter scores that measure customer retention and loyalty over time. American Express, Verizon, Costco, and others post their customer-value data in their reports to shareholders. At StitchFix, functions such as marketing, IT, supply chain, and finance are organized into teams aligned around common customer-experience targets. This online, subscription-based apparel retailer allows customers to return goods after trying them on, something that would be difficult to execute if the functions were measured on their own siloed performance (Markey, 2020). Taken together, customer-centric measures enable companies to understand important behaviors of customers at every touchpoint in the business process.

In Chapter 4 we examined the "business handshake," which can be illustrated with a grid that shows center-led product or category management teams partnering with regions or shared sales channels, as shown in Figure 7.2. Metrics should be defined for this partnership, assuring that the collaborative output is measured as a whole. Effective partners in this "business/market" partnership are then motivated to work together to set joint targets for growth, profitability, and market share. They can then utilize those metrics in a shared dashboard to co-manage their franchise. As Figure 7.2 illustrates, some cells in the grid receive more attention than others, due to their extraordinary value-creating potential.

Figure 7.2 The business handshake at key nodes in the matrix

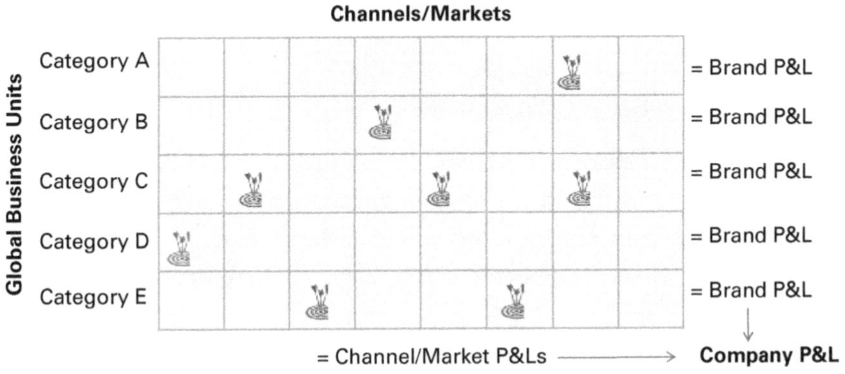

Table 7.2 Accountabilities for planning and execution

	Planning Process	**Execution/Measurement**
Global Product Management	• Define the offering • Set strategic growth goals • Develop the offering • Position the offering • Market the product	• Track profitability of the offering, globally • Identify gaps in the offering • Execute product/service support • Oversee strategic initiatives in-market
Market Unit Commercial Management	• Identify customer requirements • Set integrated market plan • Build commercial capability • Manage customer marketing • Set annual sales targets	• Execute the business plan • Track key sales and profit results by market • Measure customer performance • Manage team and individual performance

Roles in the handshake can be defined in terms of the planning work (strategy setting and annual business plans) and the execution and measurement work. Both partners have a stake in the planning *and* execution tasks, and they work together, but what each does in the handshake is uniquely value-adding, which will inform their accountabilities and the metrics that define them, as shown in Table 7.2.

Collaborative Metrics

In the networked, scaled, and agile organization, metrics must be designed with attention to two competing interests:

- Line-of-sight: Measures of a given role are highly related to those actions and decisions that the role can directly control (or substantially influence). For example, a line-of-sight metric would be rewards tied to achieving sales goals where incumbents can readily see how their performance affects the outcome.

- Collaborative outcomes: Measures owned by a team or a major part of the company that create a sense of inter-dependence among multiple roles. For example, a collaborative outcome metric would reward a team for overall results of a division where they win or fail together.

There is no right answer to this balance between individual and team metrics, and cultural factors tend to create a bias one way or the other. But there is a best blend for a given business. When incentives are attached to metrics, there is a lot of pressure to tip the balance toward line-of-sight for its perceived motivating effects and desire for clear and simple accountability. Incumbents may ask, "Why should I be held accountable for things I can't directly control? If I'm running a global product team, but the field sales organization makes the pricing decisions and manages all the customer relationships, how can I be accountable for the profitability of my products?" For decades, the reality of the matrixed organization has been that no single role controls all the elements of profitable growth in a business. Those companies that tried to run a matrix with simple line-of-sight metrics found that they were incentivizing behaviors in direct opposition to their strategy. But in the networked, scaled, and agile organization, metrics must lean even more toward "one-team outcomes."

When two or more dimensions in the matrix are designed to be more or less co-equal voices in running the business (for example, global business units and regional commercial units), many companies find it is useful to develop a collaborative P&L (Kesler and Kates, 2016). In the collaborative P&L, there are two complementary sets of financial and customer metrics. P&L targets will be composed of some that are shared by the global business team and the regional sales and service team; shared metrics are identical for each of the partners. Top-line revenue targets for product sales will be shared; a revenue target is owned by leaders in specific regions or countries; and those results will roll up worldwide to be owned by someone in a global product-management position. Revenue is a "shared metric" in this example.

But other targets will be unique to one or the other roles in the matrix, focused more on line-of-sight. These "controllable metrics" are results that one partner will have more impact on because of the nature of their role. In-region commercial leadership usually has most of the impact on the variable costs in the business, as well as the actual selling price of the offering, which translate to regional profit contribution. Global product leadership has a more unique impact on the offering and its cost of goods sold, which may be measured as gross margin, often a proforma with strategic pricing assumptions.

Figure 7.3 Controllable vs shared metrics example

	Distinct/Controllable	Shared
Global Offering	• Right global offering • Gross margin/cost of goods sold • Right global assets and tools • Ecosystem relationships • Strategic initiatives/accounts	• Revenue targets • Mix targets • Customer uptake and satisfaction • New product launch
Market Unit	• Profit contribution • Price realization • People management • Customer service • SG&A, cost of selling	• Revenue targets • Mix targets • Customer uptake and satisfaction • New product launch

There is a balance to be achieved in the way these metrics are set between line-of-sight and collaborative. The most important aspect of finding this artful balance is to avoid directly competing P&L metrics that disrupt cross-matrix agreements. A common example of this failure is metrics that place pressure on commercial regions to reduce near-term selling and administrative expenses, putting sales and marketing plans for an upcoming new product launch at risk. Another example is metrics that encourage salespeople to achieve a macro-target at the expense of profitable product mix. Figure 7.3 shows typical elements of the collaborative P&L for both partners, sorted into shared vs controllable or distinct metrics.

Defining the right organizational units for measurement is an important step in applying the *controllable vs shared* logic of the collaborative P&L. Both the vertical and horizontal organizational components must be considered. In the multi-layered, geographic example shown in Figure 7.4, the top leadership team at each level (global, region, sub-region) has a primary and a secondary measurement entity. Note that the primary in each is the greater, shared team result, and the secondary is the controllable within a given unit.

At the top, the two presidents, one for a global ventilator product and one for a region, will be measured first on company-wide performance. This metric will influence their bonus payout substantially. At the region-management

Figure 7.4 Controllable and shared metrics at each layer

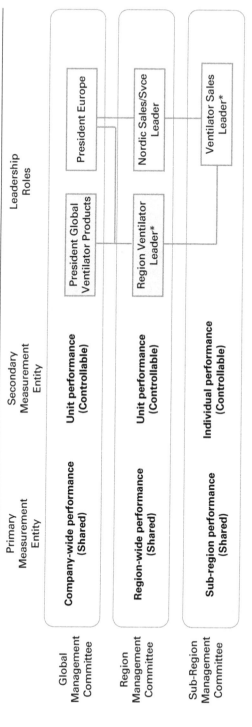

	Primary Measurement Entity	Secondary Measurement Entity	Leadership Roles
Global Management Committee	**Company-wide performance (Shared)**	**Unit performance (Controllable)**	President Global Ventilator Products / President Europe
Region Management Committee	**Region-wide performance (Shared)**	**Unit performance (Controllable)**	Region Ventilator Leader* / Nordic Sales/Svce Leader
Sub-Region Management Committee	**Sub-region performance (Shared)**	**Individual performance (Controllable)**	Ventilator Sales Leader*

*Dual reporting lines

team level, the region ventilator leader will share the consequences of region-wide performance with the Nordic sales/service leader; then, secondarily, each will be measured on separate, controllable results. A carefully crafted approach to defining metrics in this way will lead to the right leadership behaviors at all levels.

The conventional logic argues that P&Ls create accountability and if they make sense at the division level, they must also be effective for assigning responsibility for individual products and services, and for measuring manufacturing plants and sales organizations. Line-of-sight is a powerful persuader. But each entity with profit and loss accountability is an opportunity to sub-optimize performance. In its previous organizational model, Carrier Corporation's factories, each reporting to a regional president and with their own P&L metrics, provided opportunities for general managers to cover gaps in profitable sales by running positive variances or by scheduling more production than the forecasts demanded. Shifting factory measures to cost-center metrics, and managing the production footprint worldwide, eliminated waste for the company as a whole. Unnecessary P&Ls are a form of unrewarded complexity that should be avoided.

Reward Systems

Variable pay is possible when metrics are well crafted. Variable compensation can include annual bonuses as well as long-term incentives such as stock grants. Both are normally tied to achievement of defined metrics. Listen to the voices of two senior leaders, the first in a large automotive supplier, and the other in a well-known logistics company.

Automotive exec: We've talked about solutions for a long time but haven't seen the progress we want. What gets in the way is that our businesses are structured to be fiercely independent, and our compensation programs are designed to incent earnings and cash flow and almost nothing else. Our components business has the potential to deliver fully integrated, plug-and-play modules to the original equipment manufacturers. We could build door panels with integrated wire harnesses, switches, and lift motors. But there has been no incentive for the leader of the interior systems business to work with input controls, wiring harnesses, or motors to deliver a modular solution to Ford, Chrysler, or GM. Our general manager was paid to get good product to the customer, keep costs down, and keep inventories low. Delivering today paid off. Creating markets for tomorrow did not.

Logistics company exec: Compensation here is focused on operational excellence. It tracks to our advertising message. A huge portion of compensation is tied to performance metrics, and to a lesser extent financial metrics. Your pay is tied to 99.998 percent successful delivery metrics. You can hit your numbers from an operating profit standpoint but if you miss your operational performance metrics your total pay will be dramatically reduced. This focuses managers on their operational results, which is how the company differentiates itself in the marketplace. In short, hit your operational goal and your pay is doubled. Meet your P&L numbers but not your operational metrics, you could lose your job.

Pay programs are powerful messengers of what success looks like and what behaviors are expected. Rewards are a part of the Star Model and need to be adjusted to support a new strategy, operating model, or set of capabilities. A business unit that is realigned from a primarily geographic organization to global offerings will certainly change its metrics. And it will likely need to adjust the weighting of different metrics in the bonus formula to drive the new global behavior that is desired. The profit pool or organizational entity that is measured likely needs reconsideration to balance line-of-sight with collaboration needs.

Another adjustable element of a compensation system is job evaluation—placing new roles into the right pay bands. As part of an operating model change, senior roles are often substantially redesigned and may become broader. For example, a product manager role in a region assumes a global responsibility. Or, a supply chain leader, running a center of expertise for a large company, assumes operating responsibility for logistics and procurement as well. In a new operating model, a pivot role in the old organization shifts from one axis in the matrix to another.

How new jobs are evaluated for pay purposes determines the kind of candidates who are attracted to the new roles. People across the organization read these cues skillfully and will judge what is clearly valued in the pay program. When Nike shifted the center of gravity in its operating model from products to consumer categories, managers across the business were skeptical about management's determination to stay the course on such a dramatic change in the power structure. Only when heavyweight players from the legacy P&L roles were moved into these new category general management roles did it become apparent that this change was real.

Metrics for Innovation

Clay Christensen's insightful book, *The Innovator's Dilemma* (1997), compellingly characterized the impact that core business measures have on new business opportunities. The impact of the wrong metrics on innovation deserves special attention. It remains the central problem and arguably one of the greatest obstacles to growth, especially when a business faces disruption. Imagine the metrics that must have been in place, and the conversations that were happening, while Kodak was slowly overcome by the digital technology that one of its own engineers had created back in 1975.

Consider consumer-packaged-goods (CPG) companies that develop creative new product ideas after extensive use of customer data to generate insights. We have worked with great marketing-oriented CPG companies that can create these growth ideas but struggle to get them to market. The profit margins on the core businesses are often more attractive because they reflect fully depreciated capital equipment. Breakthrough innovation, in contrast, nearly always requires different production processes and a different sales force, which require capital and skills investment, negatively impacting the cost of goods sold and driving up overhead expense. The Coca-Cola Company famously sold off its bottling plants decades ago to minimize investment in capital. But when the company began to launch numerous new beverage ideas in the first decade of the 2000s, many of the bottlers were not prepared to invest the capital, regardless of the growth potential of new products. The company chose to re-acquire many of the bottling companies in order to ensure that the necessary investments were made in bottling capacity. Later, after investments were completed, they returned ownership of most of the operations to franchise partners.

Geoffrey Moore has written about the impact of negative operating margins that disruptive innovation brings to a company's profitability, and the importance of sheltering new products from the destructive effects of P&Ls and return-on-asset measures (Moore, 2015). Sub-scale, new growth franchises must be measured more on the basis of metrics such as product viability, customer enrollment, new supply chain relationships, and ecosystem partner engagement. Sales force measures and compensation can have a very big impact, too. The productivity of the selling effort tends to be lower on new products, and without intense sales training, focus, and time spent, new product launches are rarely effective. Salespeople must be measured accordingly; in some cases, a focused and possibly very costly sales team is likely to be necessary for a disruptive innovation to succeed. This will mean separate metrics that emphasize new customer relationships, market development, and customer acceptance of the new product.

In today's digital business, the power of externally focused measurement drives real-time changes in tactics, marketing assets, and even products. Today's e-commerce organizations track not only daily web traffic, but real-time figures on web landing pages, time spent on specific pages, new users, and clicks through to specific online product displays, conversion rates, and other online behaviors that correlate with daily sales increases. The data generated from these metrics are further analyzed to inform new growth trends and ideas. Profitability, cost, and return on investment metrics must be avoided in these contexts.

Key Takeaways

- Accountabilities must reflect the assumptions of the operating model if they are to align behavior with the intentions of the strategy.

- Developing the right metrics is a means of clarifying roles. When we define a purposeful pattern of metrics across a set of roles, both vertically and horizontally, we are designing an interlocking system.

- Reward systems are the manifestation of individual and team metrics and communicate what time horizon, collaboration behaviors, and decision trade-offs should be made.

References

Christensen, C M (1997) *The Innovator's Dilemma*, Harvard Business Review Press, Brighton, MA

Harris, M and Tayler, B (2019) Don't let metrics undermine your business, *Harvard Business Review*, September–October. https://hbr.org/2019/09/dont-let-metrics-undermine-your-business (archived at https://perma.cc/6L93-BYXM)

Kesler, G and Kates, A (2016) *Bridging Organization Design and Performance: Five ways to activate a global operating model*, John Wiley & Sons, Inc, New York

Markey R (2020) Are you undervaluing your customers? *Harvard Business Review*, January–February. https://hbr.org/2020/01/the-loyalty-economy (archived at https://perma.cc/KT2V-TL92)

Moore, G A (2015) *Zone to Win: Organizing to compete in an age of disruption*, Diversion Books, New York

Schuster, M and Kesler, G (2011) Aligning rewards systems in organization design: How to activate the orphan star point, *People and Strategy*, 34 (4), 34–44

Leadership and Culture

Leadership and Culture

Any book about organization is incomplete without a discussion of leadership and culture. Great leaders can thrive in any environment. By definition, learning-agile leaders can succeed under extraordinarily difficult, chaotic, uncertain circumstances. But leadership roles, skills, and behaviors exist within a social system. When leader roles are defined in a way that fits the design of the organization and when expectations are consistent with the operating model, more incumbents are likely to do well. We are far more likely to succeed in building a deep and wide bench of ready-now leaders if we consider leadership selection, development, and staffing in the context of the operating model of the company.

Culture is closely related to leadership. The characteristics of a desired culture can be described, defined, and envisioned. But culture is only changed when the social system in which leaders make decisions and model behavior is changed. The points on the Star Model that we use to design the organization system—strategy, structure, process, metrics, rewards, and people practices—are the same toolbox for shaping culture. When a future culture is articulated in a corporate growth strategy and built into the capabilities we seek to build, culture becomes an explicit part of organization design. Consider these design choices and the impact each has on culture:

- a growth strategy that emphasizes innovation, as well as reliable profit performance
- flat organization structures, with wide spans of control, and clearly defined horizontal networks and teams
- common processes and ways of working, designed around the customer and aligned against one customer experience
- profit measures that track cross-boundary team and individual performance

- incentives that drive customer focus and risk-oriented innovation
- leader selection, performance achievement, and promotion criteria that reward collaborative behaviors

Cultures transform when a critical mass of leader behaviors change, converging around a shared set of norms. Cultures and leaders can both be developed, and they are both more likely to grow to their potential if they are considered together and are built through deliberate organization design. Individual leaders learn and grow through a developmental cycle in much the same way that cultures can evolve. Mapping a change journey for both leaders and culture is a powerful way to lay out the task.

In this chapter we will focus on three aspects of leadership and culture that support a networked, scaled, and agile organization:

- aligning leadership roles to the operating model
- the development journey of leaders and cultures
- growing interdependent collaborators through the organization design process

Aligning Leadership Roles to the Operating Model

The work of leaders has to match the operating model you are designing. Therefore, there is no ideal leadership profile or set of motivations or behaviors. We have seen what happens when a high-performing, experienced executive is brought into a company without a clear match between the skills of the individual and the expectations of the company.

For example, a marketing executive is hired into a loosely related portfolio company to build a customer relationship management system, consolidate agency relationships, and harmonize core brand messages. The individual believes, however, that they are coming as a chief marketing officer to create a global, connected marketing organization. As they start to get involved in the operational decisions of the business unit and geography-based marketing units they are surprised at the push back. Offers of help are rejected. Invitations to participate on design teams are ignored or delegated. Good ideas fall flat. The marketers in the operating units are annoyed and the corporate executive is frustrated. Often, they move on within 18 months. This is not a failure of the individual. This is a failure of matching talent to organizational work. In this section we will look at leadership work through the lenses of the operating framework, vertical organization, and horizontal organization.

Operating Framework

Thinking about leadership starts right with the operating framework discussion at the top of the operating model. The role of the corporate leadership team will vary depending upon the operating framework that governs the relationship of the business portfolio.

When the CEO chooses to shift the operating model to a closely related portfolio from a more loosely connected one, and expects greater synergies across businesses, they are deciding to shift the roles and routines of leadership teams at all levels. The shift can be significant. As one moves to the left on the framework, individuals who had previously come together as colleagues to share business updates must now work together as a formal team, grappling with competing priorities, debating policy, co-creating strategy, and aligning on substantive operating decisions. One of our clients likened the feeling to going from an athlete being on a team but competing individually to suddenly having to play a team sport. They noted that "we had to learn to kick the ball and stop kicking each other." Individual excellence remains important, but shared success becomes more so.

The role and work of the leadership team will vary with each framework choice, as summarized in Figure 8.1.

As we move across the operating framework, from right to left, the roles tend to be additive. The holding company/conglomerate model requires the least amount of integration across business units, and therefore requires the minimum amount of work by the leadership team together. The work of the corporate leadership team becomes more concerted and interdependent as the degrees of required integration across the business unit increases, with the fully integrated business operating model demanding the most from the combined efforts of the executive team:

- Holding company/conglomerate: The top team is primarily focused on financial governance and maximizing returns from the separate businesses in the portfolio. They oversee enterprise reputation and risk, and in some cases may move a few business resources across boundaries.

Figure 8.1 Leadership work across the operating framework

	1 | Fully Integrated Single Business	2 | Closely Related Portfolio	3 | Loosely Related Portfolio	4 | Holding Co or Conglomerate
Exec Team Remit	Run the company together	Manage a core strategy and complementary portfolio of businesses	Optimize discrete synergies across units to generate corporate value beyond the sum of the parts	Maximize the financial returns from the assets
Exec Team Type	Strategy Setting and Operating Team	Strategy Alignment and Management Synergy Team	Portfolio Management Team	Financial Governance Team
Work of the Executive Team	• Co-creates enterprise strategy • Runs the business—manages results • Makes operating decisions	• Approves important decisions taken by separate leaders • Actively identifies linkages among business • Allocates capital • Sets annual operating plans and measures results • Oversees succession planning and talent movement practices	• Debates business portfolio options • Focuses on high-level strategic decisions • Shares best practices • Oversees corporate governance functions and reviews recommendations from committees • Reviews top executive talent	• Debates overall company philosophy, vision and issues that impact company reputation • Reviews and approves asset disposition and capital proposals • Network building among top executives • Sets tone for external relations

Additive

- Loosely related portfolio: Here top leadership may play a more active role in business portfolio oversight, seeking to drive a few key organizational synergies in order to generate corporate value beyond the sum of the parts. These are typically shared technology and other platforms.

- Closely related portfolio: In this choice leadership is defining and overseeing the core strategies of the company, harmonizing business decisions across the portfolio, and actively managing common cross-business systems, platforms, and resources. They are focused on shared capabilities and actively engaged in trade-off investment discussions.

- Fully integrated single business: Finally, in the fully integrated business the top leadership is an operational team that goes beyond oversight to actively running the company together.

The complexity and maturity of the business portfolio may also influence the work of the leadership team. The top team of a loosely related portfolio that has a mix of large legacy businesses and high growth start-ups with very different business models will have a different conversation than one that is overseeing a set of similarly sized units at similar places in their maturity. For example, in a CPG company we work with, leaders of the more mature businesses are expected to provide specific levels of support to young growth businesses. This is done through frequent talent conversations across the executive committee, where they actively seek opportunities to bring experienced leaders into the less mature businesses. The focus is on bringing in enterprise know-how to solve technical issues.

Leadership in the Vertical Organization

In Chapter 4 we argued the importance of ensuring unique, value-adding roles for each layer, avoiding overlaps in the work. The construct of strategic, integrative, and operational layers applies across the choices in the operating framework, but work will differ at each level.

Too often, we find executives working at too low a level in the organization—that is, doing some of the work of the integrative or even the operational layer. This can happen for a variety of reasons. In more mature companies it is often born out of a legacy culture of control and low tolerance for risk and failure that served the organization well as it scaled and routinized work. Senior leaders, feeling a strong sense of accountability, may get involved in work and decisions way below their pay grade. Every level feels a strong need to stay informed and to make sure important work is done right.

When executives work below their level, teams are not empowered, important senior work is neglected, and role confusion may cascade through the levels. An affirmative expectation that managers should know the details of their business becomes a value that translates into micro-management throughout the system. It becomes the culture. Cause and effect is difficult to sort, but everyone gets the message.

In younger companies the reasons are typically different but micromanaging behaviors can be similar. In high-growth companies the division of labor between layers is new and executives have not yet adjusted to the leadership work required in a bigger and more complex company. Their own development may not have matched the pace of company growth. Feeling uncomfortable with these new expectations drives them to retreat to what they know and do best—the day-to-day work of running the business.

Regardless of the reason or circumstances, the negative consequences of top executives not working at the right level are three-fold:

1 The work of the strategic layer is neglected. Because only the executives can do this work for the company, if they are spending their time on other issues lower in the organization on a routine basis, strategic muscle is under-developed. When time and attention is not spent managing the growth horizons and innovation portfolio of the company a typical consequence is insufficient strategies for horizons 2 and 3 work.

2 The integrative and operational layers are not fully empowered. Empowerment is not just a value or a feel-good objective. Under-utilized capacity in lower leadership levels means the company is not tapping the energy and expertise of the next generation of leaders. These are the people that will fuel the next wave of growth in the company. When a generation of growth leaders doesn't understand or is unwilling to delegate, they demotivate top performers and become a force for atrophy rather than growth.

3 Executive successors are under-developed. Another result of executives not working at the right level is expertise and performance gaps between the executive team and their direct reports. No matter how talented the executive bench is, if they don't get to make significant business decisions and aren't entrusted with mission critical work, they can't get ready for the next level of leadership. Not only does this imperil the leadership continuity of the company, but it often materially impairs the growth plan. And, the bench never seems to get deeper in companies of this nature. We have witnessed it limit a corporation's ability to grow through

acquisition and geographic expansion simply because there aren't enough internal senior leaders ready for that next-level challenge.

Here are some ways that organization design wisdom can keep leaders working at the right level:

1 Broaden spans of control. The more direct reports someone has and the flatter their organization is, the less likely they have time to meddle in the work of others. This is a forcing mechanism to create focus on leading versus doing.

2 Define clear governance forums. We can design decision-making forums, such as demand and supply planning, and product planning, in ways that push decisions down in the organization, closer to the customer. Entrust the work of managing the day-to-day operations, executing against agreed upon priorities, and overseeing cross-unit initiatives to the leadership teams beneath the executive level, with clear escalation guidance.

3 Measure leadership performance. Define select individual and executive team metrics in a way that links them to critical outcomes in the work of the strategic layer. For example, a growth plan with strategies defined across multiple horizons will change the conversation. Or having the strategic layer manage a diverse innovation portfolio shifts focus from near term operational concerns that are better delegated to others.

4 Select and promote leaders with learning agility. Learning agility is a personality quality that tends to be "hard-wired," and less likely than other qualities to be able to be developed. Leaders with strong learning agility are naturally inquisitive about other areas of the organization and what is new. Growing with the company and continuously working at a new level requires senior leaders to be agile learners, able to leverage what helped them to be successful at lower levels of the organization, let go of old accountabilities, and proactively embrace new ones as the company requires them to take on new challenges.

Leadership in (and for) the Horizontal Organization

Senior Leaders

For an organization to be both scaled and agile, the team at the top must be the most horizontal team in the company with each member trusting their peers to run their businesses and functions in the interest of the greater team.

An agenda that requires the top team to work together on building new growth capabilities ties them together.

When the top team's role is clear, they can focus on empowering the horizontal networks across the organization. It is impossible in any matrixed structure for a cross-boundary network of global and regional leaders to stack hands on a shared marketing and sales plan if their bosses second-guess decisions the team has made.

Top leaders create an environment of both high expectations and trust for cross-boundary teams. They can do this in several ways. Here are a few:

- Role model interdependency at the top.
- Manage an inclusive strategy process that horizontal teams can engage in.
- Set targets that can only be met through collaboration, and make it clear the cross-boundary team is accountable for results. It's not an extracurricular activity.
- Create development moves for talented people to work in diverse geographies, functions, and businesses, and reward those who seek out lateral job moves.
- Listen. Really listen to understand where the horizontals are working well and where there are continued cultural and practical obstacles that must be tackled.

The boundaryless organization has been an aspiration for thirty years (Ashkenas, Ulrich, Jick, and Kerr, 1995). The reality is that any organization with more than one team has boundaries. Like hierarchy, boundaries in human systems at scale are necessary. It is more realistic, and less frustrating, to accept and even embrace these boundaries because they allow for identity, focus, and specialization. Then, make it the work of leaders to connect purposefully across these boundaries to create value.

Senior leaders in the integrative layer are the stewards of servant leadership, writ on a grand scale. This is the integrative layer that turns the traditional, status-oriented pyramid of power on its head and brings the full value of the company to the customer. For example, business reviews still occur and the role of senior leaders is to help horizontal teams learn by coaching them in real time versus waiting for calendared presentations. The question changes from "What did you accomplish?" to "How can we help you grow your business faster?" In companies that have mastered a critical mass of agile teams, the measurement process builds trust by breaking complex tasks down into smaller parcels and sprints that can be reviewed quickly and transparently. Unless a team is clearly off the track, rule one for the senior leaders is, "Noses in, fingers out."

Leaders in the Horizontal Networks

The work of leaders who manage and work in horizontal teams is often to focus first on the customer, internal or external. The more the strategy calls for customer solutions pulled from assets embedded across the organization, the more important strong, focused, horizontal leadership becomes. This is fundamental for cloud-enabled organizations to thrive. Companies that invest in cloud and do not break down barriers for collaborating across the organization experience only minimal benefits. An end-to-end view of the business process is critical. Silos within the IT organization, and between technology in the back-end and the front-end customer-facing organization, strangle opportunities to connect to customers and enable speed, agility, and innovation across the business process. To truly leverage a revolution in digital business, behavioral and organizational change is needed. As one technology executive argued, "moving to cloud and using the same organization constructs and the same leader behaviors with all the old handoffs and barriers both within IT and between IT and the business is like getting a new Ferrari to drive on cobblestone streets."

Paradoxically, leaders of horizontal networks have less formal authority, and must rely more on compelling ideas and the ability to influence, align, and build community. Those who lead a team of teams must be prepared to bring the center-led concept to life. Across the boundaries they have to build a common agenda rooted in company vision, purpose, and strategy, with a clear picture of what the customer expects and what makes the brand relevant. They align others to shared ways of working, find ways to make decisions as one team, and show consideration toward those who co-own the business results.

Cross-boundary leaders muster influence through knowledge, energy, vision, and persuasive communication (including listening), to coalesce specialized skills and diverse assets, weaving them together into the work of networked teams that deliver outcomes that are both agile and scaled.

The Development Journey of Leaders and Cultures

As the business strategy grows more complex, requiring stretch across many diverse assets of the company to bring a customer solution to the market, the work of leaders changes as well. Because a critical mass of leader behavior change is required before we see a change in culture, it is important to consider the logic—the mindset—that underlies individual leader behaviors, as well as cultures.

To be effective in the agile, scaled, and networked organization, the leader's thinking must be equal or superior to the complexity of the environment in which they serve. And collectively the culture must reinforce those ways of thinking and behaving.

Stages of Leader Development

One provocative theory of leadership development for today's organization argues that we can map the growth cycle of the individual leader and the culture together and then design, simultaneously, for the development of both. The Center for Creative Leadership's development-stages model combines the work of Harvard's Robert Kegan and Lisa Laskow Lahey with CCL's John McGuire and Gary Rhodes. To bring about deeper development, one must first understand these stages of thinking abilities, or mindset, that exemplify individual and cultural choices and behaviors, and plot a course to advance to the next level of development (McGuire and Rhodes, 2009).

Culture change is both personal and organizational, because it starts with individual commitments that collectively become a social system. The framework presents three levels of development that leaders and cultures can aspire toward:

1 dependent conformer

2 independent achiever

3 interdependent collaborator

A list of some of the characteristics of each stage of development, with an eye on both individual leaders and collective culture, creates some sharp contrasts.

Stage 1: Dependent conformer

- team player
- specialist
- faithful follower, belonging is important
- reliant on authority

- believes knowledge is at the top
- needs direction and clear boundaries
- aligns with others

Stage 2: Independent achiever

- independent thinker, self-directed
- obsessed with execution—achieving is everything
- knowledge is power
- compete and win
- take a stand for what you believe
- guided by internal compass

Stage 3: Interdependent collaborator

- interdependent thinker
- determined the team will win
- see systems, patterns, and connections
- comfortable with uncertainty
- able to create new strategies and business models
- learns from successes and failures
- holds multi-frame perspectives and contradictions (short and long term both matter)

The outcome of this progression of development is the ability to think in more complex, systemic, strategic, and interdependent ways. Developing from one stage to the next is both an individual and a social process. When leaders in the same company practice together it produces better outcomes. Designing the organization with an activation mindset is a wonderful task for this purpose.

Leaders who progress to interdependent collaboration make connections both vertically and horizontally. They are the organizational architects who recognize that influence depends on their ability to make these connections among leaders and the nodes in the matrix. They are energized by the challenge. Leading across a broader ecosystem merely adds to the opportunities to bridge value-creating people and teams. For community-builders it is exhilarating work.

Managers who fail to take the developmental step to the next level, together, leave themselves and the culture of the company stranded.

Trust is the Bond

Trust is the bedrock of agile and networked organizations. Without trust there is no empowerment through the vertical layers of the organization and there is no true collaboration among horizontal partners, with whom one must work to bring real solutions to customers.

Perhaps like learning agility, the ability to build trust with others is more of a hard-wired trait among leaders. But there are specific behaviors that can be demonstrated by individuals to build trust with others, even among those for whom this does not come naturally. And, again, when leaders practice and model new behaviors together—even if they are uncomfortable—the culture begins to change.

Collaborative organizations run on trust. The right structure, processes, technologies, and reward systems are necessary, but not sufficient to activate a complex organization. Always there are boundaries that must be overcome. High-trust relationships are the threads that weave together the organization across these boundaries.

Social capital is built through conscious, purposeful, and informed effort. Let's look at some of what we know about trust in organizations:

1 Trust develops naturally in small units. According to the anthropologist Robin Dunbar, people can really only really know and maintain relationships with about 150 people (Dunbar, 2010). Based on this, Bill Gore famously limited the size of his manufacturing plants at Gore to 150 associates. Even with all the technologies that connect people and help them maintain relationships that have been developed since Dunbar's rule was established in the early 1990s, humans have not evolved in this matter. Knowing this, leaders can help trust develop by creating manageable units to which people feel they belong. These should not be clans with rigid norms that shun outsiders, but rather welcoming families that allow for and encourage connections with other families. This is a building block of the vertical structure and network concepts we've discussed—the idea that someone can be part of two or more "families" helps information, innovation, and decision-making to flow across boundaries.

2 Trust takes time to build. One of the benefits of stability in an organization is that people have the time to invest in relationships. When you restructure an organization, all of the existing networks are thrown into chaos and relationships have to be rebuilt in accordance with the rules of the new operating model. The goal of leaders should be to accelerate the rebuilding of critical connections, so that the organization can fully perform, on scale, as soon as possible.

3 Trust creates speed. Speed matters. Fewer steps in processes, less checking of others' work and approval of others' decisions, and fewer people in meetings and decision-making make things run more quickly. Trust is essential to eliminating non-value-creating complexity and costs in organizations, both large and small.

4 Trust happens when someone takes a risk. There is an important relationship between risk and trust. High-trust relationships start with one person taking a risk. For example, one party may conclude, "I believe you have our shared best interests in mind so I will let you take this decision for us." If they take the gamble, and the faith is not betrayed, they will engage in trusting future interactions with this person. Individuals learn to trust this way, and so do broad segments of a workforce. Beneath every major change initiative lies murky tensions between the past, the present, and the future. Risks to careers, security, and status in the organization are perceived and real, and how those risks are managed matters.

The 4 Cs of trust is a simple model that guides leaders to action. It's based on the premise that although people experience trust in different ways, there are four sets of behaviors that increase the likelihood that trust will be built with others over time (Mayer, Davis, and Schoorman, 1995):

- Commitment: You make a promise and you keep it. Not just once, but multiple times. In today's highly competitive, pressured business environments, leaders who commit to clear outcomes and then deliver them have a leg-up in building social capital. Others are drawn to these people and seek them out for their teams and their most difficult assignments. In working across boundaries, those who hedge and are reluctant to commit are more likely to be second-guessed.

- Candor and consistency: You say what you mean. And people can predict how you are going to react in a situation because you are consistent. We all know people who have expressed support for an idea or a course of action while in the room with a group of people, only to express cynicism in private conversation once the meeting is over. Those who speak with courage, even bluntly, and remain true to their views tend to have a positive balance in their influence account.

- Competence: You ensure that you and your team have the ability to deliver on your commitments, and there is a track record of accomplishment. Nothing produces more confidence, under fire, than this one. Individuals who seek feedback and are motivated to learn continuously tend to do better on this factor. Change leaders who inherit teams with troubled reputations for "delivering the goods" often must take concrete action to upgrade these teams. Distrust and cynicism grow when these weak spots are ignored.

- Consideration: You take time to understand others' objectives and convey, through dialogue, that you care about what keeps them up at night. In the horizontal, networked organization understanding the challenges that your colleagues are trying to manage is fundamental. Trust grows among horizontal teammates when one takes the extra time to understand, and then adjusts their own plan to accommodate others' interests.

Trust can be built at scale when an extended leadership team practices these behaviors with each other. Using the same model allows them to use common language and facilitates a social contract that goes something like this: "We agree on these standards, now let's put them to work. I will tell you when you are modeling the right behavior, and I expect you to do the same for me. When we invite that feedback, we have just taken a risk, and we will demonstrate we are worthy of the trust that will follow."

Growing Interdependent Collaborators Through Organization Design

Jay Galbraith once told us that you can't pull off a third-generation strategy with a second-generation organization and first-generation leaders. Did he mean you can only transform an organization if you first change out all the leaders? There is an alternative.

Moving a leadership team through the CCL model's development stages requires practice, and when leaders practice together, with similar challenging, purposeful experiences, new behaviors and skills converge around a new purpose, and the culture can change.

We have talked extensively in the last seven chapters about designing and activating scaled, agile and networked organizations. But who leads the work of defining a new company operating model? Who sets the rules of engagement for the tower and the square? When fresh thinking is required to design a new organizational system, an executive team, as well as managers and individual contributors, lower in the organization, can work together in a developmental experience for both the individuals and the company culture.

Senior executives must act as the chief organizational architects for their company. The major design decisions should not be delegated, even when the culture is highly inclusive and the design process highly participative. The role of the top team is to set the organization vision and make the primary design choices that will enable the company to deliver its long-term growth plan. They should be adept at recognizing when operating models have reached the end of their useful life, identifying organization barriers to scale and agility, championing the journey to rethink their organization, and ready to make the tough choices.

But top leaders can enroll a critical mass of the leadership organization into a process of discovery and learning, by engaging them in rethinking the organizational model. In doing so, they create a shared development experience, practicing new ways of thinking about customers, growth, talent, and the effective use of resources. Here's how to develop organization, culture, and leaders simultaneously through the design process itself:

- Use a cross-section of change leaders (100, 200 or more) to be part of building out the detailed design once the top team has set the basic architecture and design objectives.

- Use agile methods to ask teams to come back with iterations of design thinking, then challenge and blend the ideas of multiple teams through vigorous debate and sharing of data.

- Bring customers into the design sessions and ask them to provide blunt feedback on what could be better in the existing customer experience.

- Be explicit about the criteria used to judge the work, always keeping it connected to the growth strategy and the culture that will bring it to life.

- Create ownership, intimacy, and candor within and across design teams (and practice the 4 Cs of trust through the process of design).

- Model new cultural attributes (for example, innovation, decision-making speed, inclusion, or collaboration) through how the design process is structured and run.

- Use the new operating model to set a different leadership talent strategy, and hold up demonstrated, new success behaviors for all to see.

A road map can help ensure the design process builds leaders and culture together, as shown in Figure 8.2. The model lays out the role of leadership teams at each stage of the organization reinvention process. Once the top team is aligned on the business direction, then it must identify and prioritize the removal of organization barriers to deliver the new growth plan. Without top team alignment on why the status quo is no longer an option, the rest of the organization will not change.

Figure 8.2 Role of leadership teams across the design process

	STRATEGY	CASE FOR CHANGE	OPERATING MODEL	ORGANIZATION DESIGN	ACTIVATION
Top Leadership	• Set the company strategy and define the portfolio of businesses • Define the culture of the future • Charter teams to explore new growth ideas	• Define the core problem to solve with broad input, internally and externally	• Set the operating framework and the basic organization model • Get inputs on the options from leaders across the organization	• Define the structure of the business units and enterprise functions • Engage a broader team in building out the organization	• Set the implementation plan • Stay the course— keep attention drawn to full activation
Extended Teams	• Bring market and competitive intelligence forward • Participate in teams to develop growth ideas and models	• Provide input to senior leaders • Understand the case for change, wearing an enterprise hat	• Understand the proposed new model and provide input • Help to build out the details of the model	• Participate in design teams to build out the full structure, redesign business processes, ways of working, metrics and people practices • Engage the workforce around change imperatives	• Learn new leader behaviors • Continue to participate in activation activities • Listen to the workforce • Provide continuous feedback to top leaders

Once the problems to solve are clear and owned by the leadership team, then they are ready to design their new operating model for the future. This is followed by design of the new system, adjusting all points on the Star Model across the enterprise or within select areas of the company, such as specific functions, product units, or commercial units.

Finally, the leadership team is in a unique position to use the weight of their own personal sponsorship to "complete the play"—that is, fully activate the new operating model. This requires attention to the sequencing and pacing of the organization design and implementation changes.

Key Takeaways

- There is no one right profile of a leadership team. Rather, the work of leaders needs to be aligned to the operating model.

- Leader behavior creates culture. Therefore, the development journey of leaders and cultures can be designed together, moving from dependent conformer to independent achiever to interdependent collaborator.

- Strong horizontal organizations with effective structured networks depend upon a culture of interdependent collaborators that is built on high-trust working relationships between leaders.

- The organization design process itself is the place to start growing interdependent collaborators. Choices about inclusion, the work of design teams, and decision-making processes allow for new cultural attributes to be practiced and modeled.

References

Ashkenas, R, Ulrich, D, Jick, T, and Kerr, S (1995) *The Boundaryless Organization: Breaking the chains of organizational structure*, Jossey-Bass, San Francisco
Drotter, S (2000) *The Performance Pipeline*, Jossey-Bass, San Francisco
Dunbar, R (2010) *How Many Friends Does One Person Need? Dunbar's number and other evolutionary quirks*, Faber & Faber, London
Egon Zehnder in partnership with PWC (2017) Managing high velocity change while creating value, The Indie Summit, June 4

Egon Zehnder International and McKinsey & Company (2011) *Return on Leadership: Competencies that generate growth*, February

Kesler, G and Kates, A (2016) *Bridging Organization Design and Performance: Five ways to activate a global operating model*, John Wiley & Sons, Inc, New York

Mayer, R, Davis, J H, and Schoorman, F D (1995) An integrative model of organizational trust, *The Academy of Management Review*, 20 (3), July, 709–34

McGuire, J B and Rhodes, G B (2009) *Transforming Your Leadership Culture*, John Wiley & Sons, Inc, New York

Rigby, D, Elk, S, and Berez, S (2020) The agile c-suite: A new approach to leadership for the team at the top, *Harvard Business Review*, May–June

Smith, W K, Lewis, M W, and Tushman, M L (2016) "Both/and" leadership, *Harvard Business Review*, May

Stamoulis, D (2012) *Making It to the Top: Nine attributes that differentiate CEOs*, Russell Reynolds Report

Designing for New Capabilities 09

The organization frameworks and tools that we describe in this book are durable because they are based on an understanding of systems and patterns of human behavior in groups. However, the business problems and opportunities that we apply these models to change along with the business, economic, and social context.

These next short chapters address some special topics reflecting new capabilities needed by organizations in the 2020s.

a Solutions

Solutions are all about pulling together products, services, and experiences from within and beyond the company's walls and delivering them seamlessly to a customer. A true solutions strategy requires an organization able to create structured networks across organizational boundaries for collaboration at scale. Components must be assembled to create replicable, profitable results that solve multi-dimensional customer problems. The solutions strategy requires sophisticated decision-making and leaders able to manage the global and the local simultaneously.

b Innovation

The need for companies to innovate is certainly not new. What is new is the speed with which new entrants into industries can scale ideas globally using technology and ecosystem partners, including the customer and consumer. As a result, all companies have to build capability in managing a portfolio of legacy, core businesses and internal start-ups. The challenge lies not in idea generation, but in the ability to move nascent businesses out of the incubation phase and through to profitability and productivity.

c Activation

Design-led organizational change is the way to bring complex organizational visions to life through practice, learning, and adjustment. Activation of new ways of work and decision-making often require up to two years of focused support when significant power dynamics are shifted. New connections—vertically and horizontally—need to be built. New forums and agendas have to be designed to facilitate the conversations at the organizational nodes where value is created. And leaders have to be supported in modeling the new behaviors that change culture.

We address these topics in the following chapters, illustrating how the fundamental design concepts apply to the current realities of business today.

Solutions 09a

Solutions are integrated bundles of products, services, and experiences that meet sophisticated customer needs. Here are a few examples across very different businesses:

- Philips: The global healthcare tech company has shifted from a product-oriented medical equipment provider to offering integrated hardware, services, and patient software. These solutions must be tailored to regional differences in healthcare systems around the world and integrate seamlessly into existing hospital systems.

- Mailchimp: A small but successful web-based business with market-leading email marketing tools decides to create a platform for small-business customers. The platform delivers an integrated marketing solution that includes social media, automated consumer-tailored experiences, surveys, shopping, and consulting.

- Carrier: A global conglomerate of heating and cooling equipment, refrigeration equipment, and residential and commercial security systems creates a technology-focused strategy for "intelligent building systems," an integrated offering for managing all building utilities in an open architecture.

Mailchimp is a new economy, tech native that is building on an intense customer focus to grow and expand. Philips is in the middle of a long turna-round. Carrier is the essence of old economy companies and will have to refocus investment while spinning off from its conglomerate parent company. What is consistent in all of these endeavors is the challenge of scaling customer-centric innovation. Each of these companies must do so while protecting the legacy business, the existing profit engine.

Customer-focused, solutions-oriented businesses come in different dimensions and types. Common to all of them is the imperative to create an effective customer experience. The start-point is aligning organizational resources around the entire customer journey versus touchpoints in the business process. This is a wonderful call to action for creative organization design that spans all points on the Star Model.

Organizing to deliver solutions to customers can be a difficult challenge for a company with an established history of delivering products or even services. Agility is needed to pull ideas, assets, and expertise from all parts of the company. Deep specialists have to work together to meld business models into profitable outcomes. But scale is also required. If every solution is unique and not replicable and reusable in some way, it will be hard to create profitable offerings. Finally, the network is critical to achieving the strategy. While the specialists will identify with a primary team, they must feel equally comfortable contributing to global networks that span product, geographic, and functional boundaries.

This shift is not new. IBM made the journey 20 years ago and urgently needs to do so again. The transformation to customer-solutions strategies at UPS, GE, Accenture, Philips, Siemens, and others has been underway for the past decade. Jay Galbraith wrote his seminal article on "Organizing to deliver solutions" in 2002. What is different today is the imperative for so many of the industrial giants of the 20th century to reinvent themselves. In many industries, delivering solutions enabled by digital technology is not just a strategic option, but a requirement for survival.

Enterprise Agility and the Solutions Strategy

For companies that are managing a shift to solutions, the vision is to go from stand-alone products or services to smart offerings that integrate components, technology, and services to solve complex customer problems. The rise of economic buyers, who value complete cost of ownership over product features, reduces the value of hardware product innovation. Increasingly, customers want products and services integrated into software platforms that improve workflow efficiency and movement of data within their own systems. Successful companies will provide a full suite of hardware, software, and experiences to these customers. The shift is not just to add on new offerings, but also to be able to link to the customers' existing infrastructure, and even competitors', to create a seamless ecosystem.

A major change in strategy, one that shifts the business model, will tease out a set of organization design questions:

1 How will we bring the voice of the customer into core business processes?

2 What does an integrated solutions strategy mean for the fundamental alignment of P&L business units in our company?

3 Who owns the integrated solutions platform internally (IT, R&D, engineering—or a business unit)?

4 How do we set investment priorities to make the right trade-offs between what is good for a traditional business unit and what will benefit the broader ecosystem we are trying to build?

5 How do we establish accountability across diverse new players with metrics that incent the development of platforms, software, and solutions? Who gets credit in solution sales? How do we measure contribution and progress as well as revenue and profit?

6 How do we attract and retain digital talent? How do we create and incent high-performing, collaborative, and integrated teams (especially when we have to compensate digital talent quite differently than our core technology people)?

A significant organization challenge in making this type of shift is designing in accountability while incenting collaboration. It is a tough task to find the balance between motivating the executive behaviors that will support the right decisions for the customer as well as the profit requirements of the corporation over the short- and long-term horizons. That tension breaks down into natural conflicts among the players over product development and customer priorities, scalability of tailored solutions, pricing and discounting, common standards, and sequencing investments in the technology road map.

Underlying each of these challenges is a common theme: the difference between *enterprise agility* and *business unit agility*. The temptation to focus on the agile benefits of separate, autonomous business units must be resisted in a highly integrated, solutions-oriented company. Business unit autonomy works when each business serves unique customers, through unique channels, against distinct competitors. In the world of integrated solutions, enterprise agility must be the goal, and business units actually become obstacles to enterprise agility. With its powerful, product-oriented business units, Microsoft learned this lesson. It failed to respond to changes in the market via the cloud and handheld computing until the enterprise model was shifted from products toward a more agile and project-oriented structure. Its return to market leadership with this new model has been extraordinary.

Symptoms of Misalignment

We see six common internal obstacles to making the shift from a product-oriented company to a solutions company:

1 The autonomous nature of product-oriented business units does not provide any point of accountability for replicable and scalable customer solutions. Product lines focused on their own profitability don't have an interest in the give and take necessary for configuring solutions.

2 The proliferation of P&Ls is simply too complex. Leaders feel exhausted by the effort needed to agree on plans. The investment of energy needed for alignment takes away from being out in the market with customers.

3 Power relationships among the business units, markets, and functions are not designed from the voice of the customer back. Customer-centric is an empty word until backed up by decision guardrails that tip outcomes to the customer and the long-term, away from short-term business unit goals.

4 Innovation is still triggered by technology and product push, rather than starting with the customer and the market. This inhibits ideas that serve distinct areas, connected by a single platform across boundaries.

5 The sales organization is not ready to fully build consultative relationships, and the metrics and incentives for cross-functional, customer-centric teams haven't been figured out.

6 The cost structure is weighing down the ability to reinvest in innovation. Corporate costs and headcount still reflect a multi-segment business, and energy is not available to be directed to new capabilities.

Organizational Building Blocks

Solution strategies are often seen in the closely related operating framework. Such businesses can have portfolios with six or more dimensions that can contribute to a given customer solution:

- products
- services, consulting, and training
- customers, segments, and channels
- geographic markets
- platforms
- functions and systems

In the solutions-focused organization, each dimension has a role to play and the relationship and power balance must shift.

Products

The traditional organization is built around product business units, each with a distinct P&L. Even if support functions or operations are shared, these business units usually operate with separate product development groups and have decision authority for discrete offerings.

In a product company, the business units design and develop, and the commercial market organizations sell and deliver. In a solutions business, the product and service groups create the components, designed to fit together as prototypes. In software terms, these are "solution architects." The markets identify opportunities and configure customer-specific solutions built on the prototypes. In software language, the market leads are "system integrators." They serve as the project delivery executives, selling a plan for growth to the customer.

With the solutions strategy, the classic business units evolve into product and service component developers, creating hardware and software components that can be deployed into multiple solutions. These components are highly reusable, but also customizable by the market for customers, with the right balance of standard and unique characteristics. This is a difficult capability to develop but foundational to the solutions strategy and profitability.

To make this practical, the business unit dimension should include as few P&L centers as possible and should be tightly focused on customer-centric innovation. Accountability should be focused on the overall results of the company as well as the effectiveness of specific components in the marketplace.

Services, Consulting, and Training

In product companies, services may be delivered as separate offerings, with distinct P&Ls, or they may be considered as loss-leader add-ons to create more value for the product. Typical services include consulting, workflow design, and outsourcing, as well as traditional post-sale repairs, maintenance, and updates.

In solutions companies, the design and development of services become standard components that can be configured and integrated into the products. The integration is done by the market, not by the product groups. In this way, the market controls what configuration of products and services best suits the customer's needs and how to price it.

The actual delivery of services—whether professional consultation or product repair—must be managed and located close to customers to build relationships and account for language, culture, and regulatory differences. "Supply chain" is no longer just the flow of materials from supplier to customer, but includes the flow of people who consult, educate, customize, and service the customer as an integral part of the solution. This talent supply chain has to be designed to optimize customer experience and flexible use of specialized expertise. This will include a skills identification system for workforce planning and optimal deployment. These systems may be managed regionally, but usually reside on a single technology backbone to oversee a global view of talent.

Customers, Segments, and Channels

Often, solutions-oriented companies will have focus areas that are stewarded by the business units. These could be medical therapy areas (e.g., oncology or cardiology) or vertical industries (e.g., utilities, financial services, etc.).

In solutions companies these segments become a strong organizing dimension, bringing together products, services, and market insights into an end-to-end set of offerings. The interests of the customer or segment are often represented through formal integrator roles. Such roles may be individuals, lean teams that build networks across component developers and market configuration consultants, or full operating units with substantial accountability and authority.

Geographic Markets

In global companies, the geographic market units are often the point where products and services are integrated into solutions. The market's role is to localize a standard offering to be relevant to the technological and economic environment.

The market is the driver of the bundled offering to the customer. Geographic markets configure integrated, profitable solutions based on components developed by the product and service groups. The market also identifies the customers' articulated and unarticulated needs and brings these requirements upstream to inform future component development. Each company will need to create criteria to determine how to optimally group the markets around customer synergies and for efficient delivery. Solutions-delivery cannot be profitable unless the market leaders agree to work with a suite of configurations that are replicable at scale. One-off solutions are value drains on the system.

In a solutions company, not everyone sells solutions. True customer-centricity means doing business the way the customer wants. This requires a diverse sales force that can deliver a product as a simple transaction as well as a complex, consultative sale. It is not a simple shift from one model to another; it requires the roles, metrics, and systems that can support a wide range of business models in a market.

Platform

A platform is at the heart of the solutions strategy. As a company moves from product to solutions, products and services are built upon a common "chassis," not unlike today's automotive designs. In the digital-enabled solution, data architecture, workflow management, and software languages are congruent so that the solution components can talk to one another. In integrated healthcare solutions the platform may be a managed care backbone that ensures patients receive the right offering across multiple services. Regardless of the type of platform or industry, strong governance is necessary to make sure all components work fully with the platform.

Functions and Systems

In the solutions-oriented organization, each function should focus on the capabilities needed to specifically support the solutions strategy. For example, finance and IT have new critical roles in identifying and tracking costs so that complex deals can be priced and managed appropriately over the lifetime of the relationship.

Functions may serve as chief architects behind platforms. The vice president of design at Mailchimp sets the customer experience architecture across all of its component teams. In Nike's integrated marketplace, the supply chain and IT organizations must deliver inventory visibility across the retail ecosystem, including retail partners, brick and mortar, and e-commerce channels. A single invoicing system is critical. Upstream and downstream marketing, which may currently sit in the business units and the markets, has to be redesigned end-to-end.

MedSolve Case

Let's look at the example of a company we will call MedSolve. The company is a large healthcare equipment manufacturing and services company, with company-owned healthcare clinics across the US. The rise of economic buyers and price pressure in the medical device market has reduced the value of hardware product innovation and commodity medical services. MedSolve aspires to a higher value proposition with integrated, managed care solutions that reduce the total cost of care. By having more end-to-end control of patient health outcomes the company can take on more profitable provider and payer contracts that in the past would have represented higher risk.

Most of the organization components we described earlier are present in the legacy MedSolve organization: products (diagnostic and treatment equipment), services (clinics and home care delivery), customers/channels (government, insurers, hospitals, and health systems), and functions (manufacturing, quality, technology, R&D). In the legacy model, products and services were separate P&L units, each serving customers with their own go-to-market teams.

A diagnostic assessment of the existing organization was conducted, and a set of problem statements were prepared, based on the new integrated care strategy. Here is a short summary of the problem statements:

- There is no common agenda for integrated care that connects and aligns the work of existing business units.

- The current product and service lines of business do not enable integrated and value-based care. These P&L units reinforce independent operations and duplication. Leaders are focused on optimizing results within silos.

- Multiple sales, marketing, and customer management groups call on similar customers, limiting the ability to offer a consistent solution to a single call point, whether patients, providers, or payers.

- Functional duplication within business units creates role confusion, limits consistency and effective use of expertise, and does not enable effective solutions platforms. IT systems, solutioning, pricing, and other key processes remain fractured.

- The home-therapies line of business is not yet at scale and could be lost within an integrated offering.

The strategy work highlighted three different types of offering across the existing lines of business.

1 Standard (fee for service or product): Equipment, supplies, lab services.

2 Configured: Package of machines plus supplies, with customer support, lab services, and pharmacy.

3 Integrated: Managed care, value-based solution, and pricing structure with whole patient focus.

The new organization model would be constructed to enable all of these potential offerings. Working with the assessment findings, the leadership team worked through a set of design questions:

- Where do we place ownership for the customer experience, including execution of the configurable solutions?
- Where do we place ownership for development of the components of the offering (products, services, etc.)?
- Where do we place the fulfillment platforms and the shared systems and skillsets that enable profitable delivery of the offering?
- How does the definition and role of the business units and commercial channels/markets change?
- Where will the P&Ls be embedded among those dimensions, and with what metrics?
- What are the right reporting relationships? Which leaders need to be at the executive table?
- Within the functions, how do we balance the goals of operational excellence with the need to fuel innovation, experimentation, and learning?

Using these questions, the executive team began to consider a set of options for a new organizational model. Several iterations were considered, utilizing the front, middle, back modular framework. Eventually the team landed on the design shown in Figure 9.1.

The legacy lines of business were placed in the middle of the model. Their status shifted from fully integrated businesses to product and service component developers. Patient care management and navigation is an additional dimension in the middle, represented by the vertical gray bar. This

Figure 9.1 MedSolve organization model

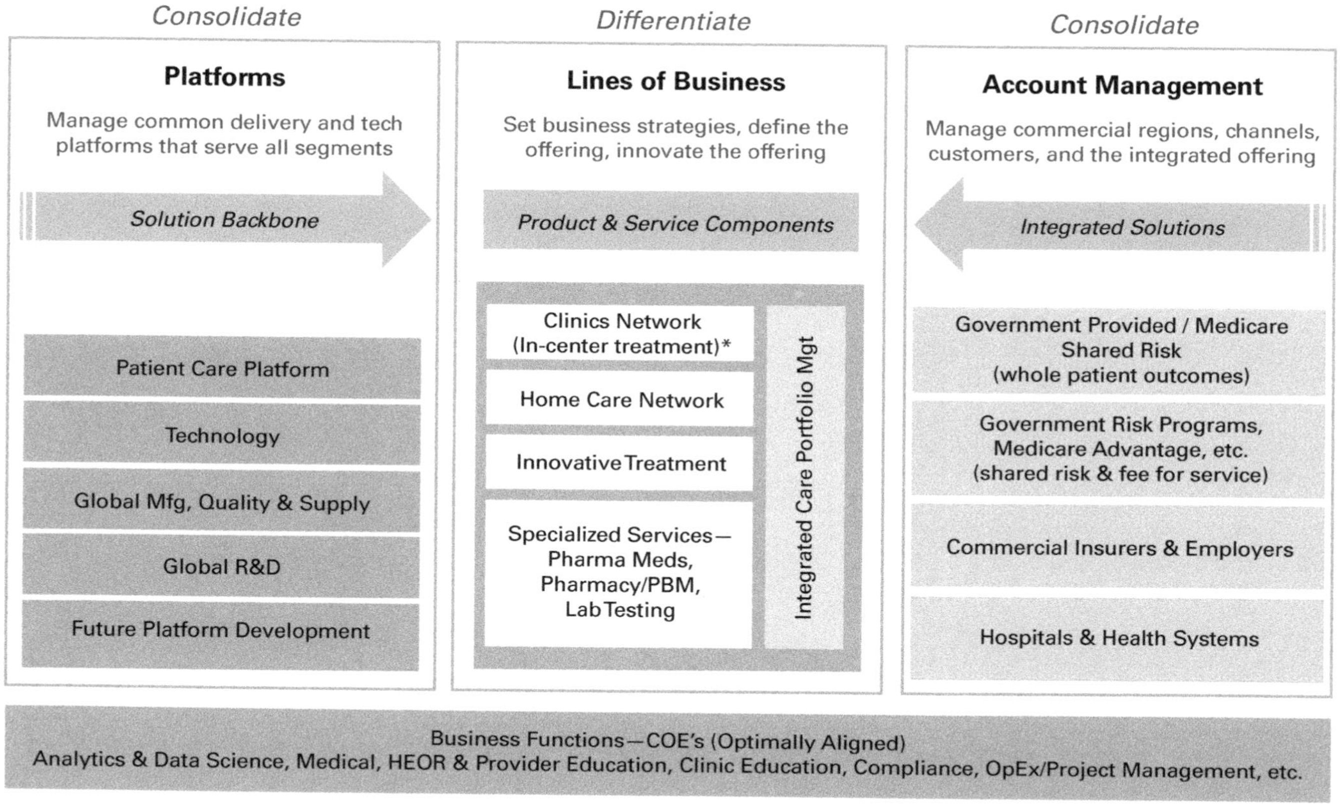

Consolidate	Differentiate	Consolidate
Platforms	**Lines of Business**	**Account Management**
Manage common delivery and tech platforms that serve all segments	Set business strategies, define the offering, innovate the offering	Manage commercial regions, channels, customers, and the integrated offering
Solution Backbone	Product & Service Components	Integrated Solutions
Patient Care Platform	Clinics Network (In-center treatment)*	Government Provided / Medicare Shared Risk (whole patient outcomes)
Technology	Home Care Network	Government Risk Programs, Medicare Advantage, etc. (shared risk & fee for service)
Global Mfg, Quality & Supply	Innovative Treatment	Commercial Insurers & Employers
Global R&D	Specialized Services— Pharma Meds, Pharmacy/PBM, Lab Testing	Hospitals & Health Systems
Future Platform Development	Integrated Care Portfolio Mgt	

Business Functions—COE's (Optimally Aligned)
Analytics & Data Science, Medical, HEOR & Provider Education, Clinic Education, Compliance, OpEx/Project Management, etc.

unit becomes the owner of the integrated care offering. It is essentially an integrator role that must influence separate component developers with a single strategy and set of customer requirements. And it is the single face to the front-end, go-to-market or account units.

The front-end of the future MedSolve organization model owns the customer. The sales force is specialized by customer type. The back-end of the future organization model is characterized as platforms, which are necessary for solution delivery. The work done by these platforms has been pulled out of the legacy business units and pooled into shared resources. In time this work will be completely reengineered, and supported with a single patient care database and digital and artificial intelligence care systems for patient monitoring and medicine management.

The business functions are captured in the model in the gray bar at the bottom, illustrated as a set of capabilities that cut across all three towers.

Once the organizational model was defined, the team could begin the task of clarifying the nature of roles and power relationships among the components. The P&L in this kind of organizational model is simplified and refocused on integrated outcomes managed by the customer-facing team in the front-end. These teams have the accountability to configure and tailor profitable solutions based on the available service and product components within the lines of business. The lines of business, in the middle, shift to cost centers but will share accountability for revenue growth and other collaborative metrics.

Rethinking the organization to deliver complex, highly integrated customer solutions is a compelling case for change that stretches the demand for agility, especially in the customer-facing parts of the business, while creating the reliability and efficiencies of scale through technology-enabled delivery components. The demands on horizontal working arrangements are the center of the challenge, and only a system-wide view of design, with attention to structure, roles, business processes, technology, collaborative metrics, and the right people practices and behaviors, will accomplish this ambitious objective.

Key Takeaways

- Solutions are offerings that bring together products, services, and experiences from within and beyond the company to solve client needs.

- Development of replicable, profitable solutions requires a high degree of integration between those who are developing the components of the offering and those who are assembling, pricing, and delivering them to the client.

- A solutions strategy challenges leaders to identify the highest value investments and make choices across the portfolio of clients and offerings, while managing the work end-to-end horizontally.

Reference

Galbraith, J R, (2002) Organizing to deliver solutions, *Organizational Dynamics*, 31 (2), 194–207

Innovation

Effective businesses listen to customers and then create great products and services that meet their needs profitably. But these same decision-making and resource allocation processes that make companies successful initially are the very same processes that then reject disruptive technologies that lead to renewal and continued growth (Christensen, 1997). In organization terms, why would any rational business unit leader, measured on profitable revenues, choose to allocate resources to proposals that will not immediately receive support from customers, can only be sold in smaller markets, and will generate smaller returns for an unknown amount of time?

The innovation problem to solve in most large companies centers on competing priorities and choices of linkage and separation. Consider Deere & Co's market-leading tractor and harvester divisions. A few years ago, new hires from Microsoft proposed working with seed and chemical companies to market proprietary big data pulled from micro-processors embedded in the farming equipment. The idea only succeeded when this new digital, data-driven business was pulled out into a separate unit. It couldn't gain traction in the core agriculture equipment business. It needed focused attention and dedicated resources. Deere's successful venture is now a case study in how product-centric firms can utilize platform-centric models to compete in the digital age (Perlman, 2017).

But seemingly agile incubation units that isolate ventures completely from the scaled capabilities of the mothership are not always a path to growing new businesses. A large European pharmaceutical company focused on developing cell and gene therapies provides an example of the organizational challenge in finding the right mix of agility and scale to house disruptive innovation teams.

Gene therapy development is often the result of extensive partnerships between academic researchers and industry practitioners that collaborate through the entire process. This typically means standing up a separate team with all business functions from research and development to commercialization, production, and supply chain management. For this company, the project began as a collaboration with a major US university. A small team worked at a location away from the main European corporate campus. As the project advanced to full development a business unit leader was assigned and provided dedicated functions for phase three clinicals and commercialization. The team built their own business and management processes.

Within months of the new product launch, problems became apparent. Scaling production was a bigger challenge than the start-up team could handle, which threatened the timeline. The corporate manufacturing group sent team members into the young cell and gene business unit. They established matrix reporting back to the central function. This, predictably, led to tensions and conflicts over decision rights and priorities in the production process. As launch of the new product began, other functions asserted their rationale for dual-reporting relationships. Within six months the business unit was dissolved, and all resources including budget control were folded back into the manufacturing, drug development, and franchise commercial organizations. The university partners were no longer included in any operational decisions. The initial product launch was successful, but alignment and control issues continued. Soon team members were spending more time debating solid versus dotted line reporting connections than focusing on the customers or the next product.

Successful innovation requires more than a good idea. Many companies are actually quite effective at identifying trends, developing new ideas, and mustering resources to bring them to life. The real challenge is scaling innovation in a sea of competing priorities. How does leadership maintain attention to disruptive programs that may not bring immediate substantial returns at the same time they are battling for market share, investing in product-line extensions, and building new off-shore routes to market in the core business? It is the essence of leadership responsibility to manage the choices among many worthwhile investment options. Govindarajan and Trimble pioneered the idea of a balance of separation and linkage back to the core for disruptive innovation over a decade ago (2010). Since then, research has provided additional insight into how to move new ideas through the growth cycle and with implications for organization design.

Innovation Across the Growth Cycle

In his book *Zone to Win*, Geoffrey Moore lays out a thoughtful framework for managing a portfolio of innovations and investments with an eye towards moving break-through, disruptive innovation through those cycles, all the way to scale and eventual maturity (Moore, 2015). Moore's work addresses how large, established companies can successfully create new disruptive innovations while profitably operating their core business. Or, as we have framed the question throughout this book, what is the best way to organize for both agility and scale in the context of disruptive innovation?

Creating and executing strategies in several strategic horizons at one time is what companies must do to continue to grow. But for many the management of breakthrough innovation in the context of a mature business is an under-developed muscle. Moore's zone offense framework provides an effective logic in this regard. Top management must focus simultaneously on four sets of competing priorities. These four "zones" are used to actively manage a progression of innovation priorities through a purposeful life cycle, pulling them back into the core at the right time, as illustrated in Figure 9.2. The four zones are:

1 Incubation: This zone is for nurturing a select number of new organic or acquired offerings or business ventures that have potential to become disruptive innovations in the longer-term. In organization terms, these investments require separation, focus, and high degrees of autonomy. They are measured with venture-funding milestones such as concept viability. Only a select few of these ventures will progress to the next innovation zone.

2 Transformation: This zone is for rapidly scaling a promising innovation with a proven market opportunity, as quickly as possible. The goal is to get this new innovation to 10 percent of total revenue within two to three years. Most companies can only manage one of these promising but fragile priorities at a time. Every area of the company must rally around and have a role in supporting the scaling of this new venture. Organizationally, these units will begin to look like vertical businesses, with considerable autonomy. They are likely to have negative returns and are measured primarily on customer uptake.

3 Performance: In time, innovations that scale successfully in the transformation zone find their way into the performance zone, the mainstream of a company's business. Organizationally, the innovation moves into the business unit structure of the firm and may fully take advantage of shared commercial and operations infrastructure. It becomes a significant source of sales and profit and fully part of the core business. It is expected to deliver profitable growth and to generate return on invested capital.

4 Productivity: Moore's framework wisely outlines a fourth zone where the priority now shifts to driving productivity. In this stage, select resources

Figure 9.2   Moore's "Zone to Win" framework

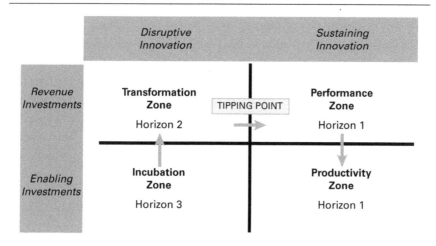

are consciously reduced so that they can be reinvested in the next new idea. Efficiency is the obligation of the fully scaled productivity business. There is no way to sustain the focus of attention and investment across competing priorities unless scaled businesses do their part to repurpose scarce resources.

As a company brings a portfolio of innovations through these zones, the organization model is likely to shift. As a set of business units enter the productivity zone, we are likely to see a front, middle, back model develop with greater sharing or consolidation of resources in the back and the front.

From Incubation to Transformation: The Organizational Challenge

Let's go back to the European pharma company trying to solve the organizational question of just how much to separate versus integrate the cell and gene therapy unit with the parent company. Without a road map, these are difficult choices that may lead to value destruction. Moore's work provides some organizational clues.

The cell and gene therapy unit needed a different business model, technology, and expertise than the core business. Programs such as this need intense focus and separation in the early going. These teams can succeed, much the way our biopharma example did, by anticipating customer needs, developing a concept, and managing the science and the technology to produce an offering that is technically and commercially viable.

It is often in the next stage in the development of the disruptive innovation that the struggles begin. The transition from the incubation to the transformation zone is surely the most difficult part of the journey. The transformation zone is not a place in the company, but a distinct leadership and organizational focus, owned at the top. Knowing when you've reached the tipping point from incubation to transformation is both art and science. All elements of the Star Model must be in balance. In our experience, an over-focus on structure without clear assumptions about linkages over time leads to most problems, not unlike in our biopharma example.

What makes the most successful innovators stand out is that they start wiring a new venture for scale while it is in the incubation zone. What does this look like? Here are some examples:

- They dedicate staff to a venture but ensure these people are also connected back to company centers of expertise.

- Existing research, data, analytics, insight development, and knowledge management platforms and tools are leveraged to bring best practices to ventures and support learning being shared back into the broader company.

- Venture sponsors are assigned as the venture moves from incubation through performance. Continuity is important but different perspectives are needed for guidance as the strategic and organization context changes over the life cycle.

Maintaining degrees of separation in the transformation zone is important, but now the new offering must also begin to benefit from the greater assets and capabilities of the company. Design of horizontal organizational elements, while retaining necessary separation, may look like this:

- Bring know-how from the core business to the new venture, while minimizing controls that are not relevant to the new.

- Give the venture its own specialized sales force, even if it seems to cost too much.

- Apply metrics that focus on pace of growth, sales and customer buy-in, and scaling efforts, rather than profits or return on investment.

Figure 9.3 Organizational evolution

	Incubation Zone (H3)	Transformation Zone (H2)	Performance Zone (H1)	Productivity Zone (H1)
	Charter: catch the next wave; demonstrate technical and commercial viability of a disruptive (H3) offering.	Charter: take the H3 idea to the market at scale and begin to benefit from the greater assets of the company.	Charter: provide returns to owners, and generate cash to to fund H2–3.	Charter: continuously improve productivity and optimize current operations, freeing up resources for disruptive innovation.
	Disruptive innovation, no appreciative revenue for years – but a **credible claim** to be the next big franchise.	Get to scale. Move quickly to become 10% of the revenue stream, in time, with superior margins.	Deliver the goods on time! Manage the stress, and keep the business model vital.	Overcome tensions with the business, free up talent and create **headroom for new investment.**
	Metrics: Venture-funding milestones (minimal viable product, clearly defined market, etc.).	**Metrics:** non-linear growth, likely negative impact on operating margins—no ratios applied!	**Metrics:** revenue, profit growth, return on investment, market share.	**Metrics:** regulatory compliance, efficiency, service metrics, systems excellence.
	SEPARATE, FULLY SPECIALIZED	**PARTIALLY INTEGRATED**	**THE CORE**	**FULLY INTEGRATED**

- The CEO and executive team actively manage the venture during this phase—leading to new conversations and possibly a forum with a sub-set of the executive team and other select voices that can problem solve quickly.

- Leaders create a culture and mindset of "What can I do right now to help accelerate your progress?" across the broader organization.

Success in shifting the new business to the transformation zone requires discipline in choosing the right timing, then attending to both the structural and the non-structural design elements of the organizational system— strategy, process, metrics, rewards, and people practices, as show in Figure 9.3.

MedDev Case

Let's examine how a high-tech medical devices company we will call MedDev chose to organize to develop a new artificial intelligence-enabled device, using the zone framework.

MedDev operates as a closely related portfolio company. Historically, MedDev robotic devices were solely focused on a variety of surgical interventions. Surgical robots convert surgeon movements into instrument movements through digital communications between a remote patient cart and a physician's console.

Its organizational model is defined by a differentiated middle, composed of product component units across robotic devices, proprietary software, and medical supplies. It is built with a consolidated back-end for R&D, manufacturing, and supply chain, and a consolidated front-end focused on sales, market access, and commercial marketing.

The new product focuses on diagnostics. MedDev uses artificial intelligence to provide real-time warnings, guidance, and advice during a procedure. This artificial intelligence-delivered guidance is built on machine-learning algorithms derived from thousands of previous cases and stored in the cloud for access when needed. MedDev has been very deliberate about dedicating focus to this incubating innovation, while maintaining soft connections to centers of expertise at the enterprise level.

A focused set of organizational elements was designed once a viable concept had been identified through a series of partnering events with MedDev surgical customers, including a practical plan and set of criteria for when the work would progress to transformation:

1 Structure: A dedicated senior business leader and team were chartered to lead all aspects of the new venture—strategy, product design and development, and commercial business development. Team members were 100 percent dedicated to the venture but maintained a strong relationship back to their respective functions (engineering, marketing, research, etc.) to maintain alignment on training and standards. This ensured the singular focus that is so critical during incubation, but also ensured that the best thinking of expert functions is being brought to bear on solving problems and removing barriers for this innovation to be successful.

2 Executive sponsorship and expert advisory structures: From the very beginning the CEO ensured that the venture leader would have a designated set of expert advisors who would be accessible through the incubation and transformation zones—notably, manufacturing, regulatory, and clinical operations. These leaders served as coaches to the venture leader and helped problem solve on product development and commercialization. These same advisors were aligned to be a steering team that made decisions about the venture's readiness to move to the next zone.

3 Shared business process: The new offering shared many customers with the core offering—especially large healthcare systems and thoracic surgeons. MedDev's deep relationship with these customers was critical to the venture team in clinical testing and in developing commercial strategies. Therefore, it made sense to leverage the regulatory process and practices of the parent company to provide a clear path to gaining necessary approvals.

4 Governance process: The CEO and his executive team govern the zone framework that MedDev has adopted. The decision to move an innovation from the incubation to the transformation zone is likely one of the highest value decisions the executive team makes every few years. To inform this decision they evaluate several things:

- New venture commercial viability: Before the new diagnostic venture was ready to leave the incubation zone, objective criteria were established to determine how readiness to proceed to the transformation zone would be judged.

- Timing: MedDev has endeavored to follow Moore's counsel that one venture at a time for most companies should be in the transformation zone. Spacing out transformation bets is essential to ensuring sufficient time and focus, from all the organization units of the business, are given to the new venture (including those that primarily play in the performance and the productivity zones).

- Organizational readiness: The executive team actively oversees key functions such as sales, market access, and marketing to determine their readiness and role in supporting the launch of the new offering.

Innovation—from continuous improvement to disruptive business model change—will remain an imperative for the established firm. The pandemic of 2020 has shown that having the capability not just to create new products and services but also to change the way in which they are delivered can make the difference in company survival. Those companies that have their organizations set up to identify needs, develop and test, and make the right connections back to the core business will be those that turn challenges into opportunities.

Key Takeaways

- The organization challenge of innovation is how to move ideas through development stages with the right degree of linkage and separation from the core business.
- Successful scaling of new ventures begins in incubation when decisions are made regarding roles, process, and metrics.
- Moore's zones framework can be adapted to help shape organization choices as innovations move from the incubation to transformation to performance to productivity.

References

Christensen, C M (1997) *The Innovator's Dilemma*, Harvard Business Review Press, Brighton, MA

Govindarajan, V and Trimble, C (2010) *The Other Side of Innovation: Solving the execution challenge*, Harvard Business Review Press, Brighton, MA

Moore, G A (2015) *Zone to Win: Organizing to compete in an age of disruption*, Diversion Books, New York

Perlman, C (2017) *Product to Platform: John Deere revolutionizes farming*, Harvard Business Review Press, Brighton, MA

Activation 09c

Activation is design-led organization change. We define it as "the deliberate and adaptive creation of new work, decisions, and business outcomes gained through the repetition and refinement of management processes and interactions over time, enabled by well-designed organizational arrangements and collaborative mindsets. Activation is the bridge from design to performance" (Kesler and Kates, 2016).

Before joining Accenture in mid-2020, we served as consultants to Julie Sweet and the Accenture leadership team. Julie became CEO in the summer of 2019 and announced the Next Generation Growth Model shortly after. She asked us to work with the leadership team ahead of the March 2020 go-live date to prepare for the launch and subsequent activation work. As we go to print, this activation work is just six months in and very much in progress. We share it here because it illustrates best practice in leadership embracing a new organization model and the hard work needed to bring it to life.

The Next Generation Growth Model

Accenture is a professional services company with over 500,000 employees. The company serves thousands of clients globally with strategy and consulting, interactive, technology, and operations services. The operating model was realigned in response to a very clear case for change. Despite attractive growth in a number of its major service areas, other services and practices had lost market share, due to the company's inconsistent track record in bringing integrated solutions to its largest and most sophisticated clients. Given Accenture's unique set of offerings, leadership saw an opportunity to bring end-to-end services across the c-suites of these clients.

The new organization is a matrix of four global service offerings that all go to market through three geographic markets, which are made up of 20 geographic market units. The global offerings include enterprise technology platform integration services, business process outsourcing, strategic consultation, and digital transformation. Within the four global service groups are sets of specialized practices, focused on capabilities such as business strategy, artificial intelligence, technology platform development, digital marketing, customer experience, and talent and organization. Each service and practice area owns a highly complex set of offerings and capabilities that come to life through closely wired connections in the three markets, where client-facing teams, staffed by professionals linked in to the four global services, live and work. These client teams in the market units are the operating layer. The system works in service of these client teams so that they are enabled to bring the right solutions to clients and deliver with speed and excellence.

The services and the markets/market units are the primary axes of the organization. A third dimension—industry networks—brings deep local and global knowledge to client teams in areas such as retail, consumer products, healthcare, banking and finance, technology, and communications. Accenture's clients expect that solutions will be informed and delivered through an industry—and in some cases a cross-industry—lens. Accenture's service, practice, and industry orientation allows for deep specialization and expertise. The goal is to integrate the right mix of specialization around a given client need, seamlessly.

Accenture's market organizations each have a full set of the ingredients that go into the client "dish," with most of its practitioners aligned to both a market unit and a global service and/or practice homeroom. Integration is to occur at a global and local level:

- The integrators at the global level include global industry leads who will build formal networks of experts to collaboratively anticipate the future direction of the industry, create global growth strategies, assemble offerings (the dish with many ingredients), and create campaigns. The leaders who run the four global services and the practice leads within, of course, are also leading networks across geographies, focused on building capabilities with the right skills and talent, the right technologies, the right ecosystem partnerships.

- The integrators in the market level include client account leads and client team leads, who must sell and deliver in a manner that allows Accenture to go to market as "one team" with clients in their geography. These integrators pull together teams of practitioners from all of the relevant services and practices with the right mix of skills and knowledge. Teams will come together around a given client for a period of time, then will re-assemble in a different configuration for another client.

Leaders in the three markets also play an integrative role, between the global and market unit layers and across market units. They translate global strategies into plans and programs that fit regional differences. And they create scale at a regional level to share scarce resources or leverage collective efforts. These market roles are particularly important to clarify in the model as they can easily devolve to span-breaking "mailboxes" moving information up and down. When well designed and brought to life with leaders that fully embrace the boundary-spanning nature of the work, the market roles help colleagues to find the sweet spot between generic global efforts and narrow local needs.

Accenture's ambition can't be delivered through a simplistic model. An overemphasis on managerial simplicity often makes people happy internally but will result in gaps for the customer and hamper growth for the company. A sophisticated strategy requires a commensurate organization. This kind of networked system requires two years or more of conscious activation to bring it to life—to create agility at scale. Trust has to be built across new working relationships. Leaders must become skilled at relying on influence—selling a compelling idea to colleagues—and comfortable working within the matrix. Metrics and reward systems must be tailored to drive collaborative decision-making, but also reward trust and letting go. At the end of the day, behavior must change up, down, and across the organization. Accenture was already a large, multi-faceted organization, with strong patterns of teamwork and collaboration. But the growth model requires new types of collaboration across more boundaries and significantly changes roles and relationships. With this degree of change, everyone must build new muscle memory.

Activation

We have argued for three broad sets of tactics to activate these complex horizontal organizations (Kesler and Kates, 2016):

- the right connections
- the right conversations
- the right leaders (and leader behaviors)

Accenture provides an effective study in the application of activation tactics in each of these categories.

The Right Connections

The vertical organization makes high-impact collaboration possible. When layers are clear, with unique contributions and no overlap, when roles are designed within the construct of the layers, and everyone understands their place in relationship to those who serve the client, then it is easy to make connections across boundaries. For example, at Accenture a critical connection is the handshake between the services and the client group leads within a market unit. Together they set priorities across the many client opportunities that will advance the shared strategy, identify the right solutions, and deliver results against the quarterly targets. Roles must be defined in the context of those partnerships all the way back up to their respective global leaders if there is to be alignment on the ground.

Additionally, threads must be woven worldwide through the industry networks, from the center all the way out to the local markets. If each market is left to create its own offering, it is impossible to create best-in-class, profitable solutions. But if the center attempts to dictate the elements and the terms of the offering completely they will miss local nuances.

Not everyone needs to collaborate, and part of activation work is assessing and learning which nodes create the most value when connected. Finding the connection points starts with the customer and the operating layer of the organization. At Accenture, these include acquiring clients, generating solutions, and delivering results. Working with a basic process view of the work, we can identify the horizontal flow and call out specific "docking stations"— standing points of collaboration that bring the operating model to life.

For example, for a large global client, global and market level industry leaders will need to wire strategy, solutions, and content together, working with practice leaders who have critical expertise in applied intelligence, process innovation, and business strategy. Explicit forums will be necessary for these groups to work intensely together with the right cadence and working practices, all in service to the global client team that must shape and deliver the solution. And, of course, each member of the client team is also a member of a service and/or a network so the alignment must be clear vertically as well as horizontally.

The process for Accenture to tailor specific solutions for clients happens within the local market unit, but the same representation of services, practices, and industry must have a formal set of connections from top to bottom. Clarity of organization coupled with process discipline is the basis for agility.

The Right Conversations

It will be a long time before a majority of complex business decisions are made by algorithm. Until then, human beings having conversations is the way that decisions are made. When an organization is redesigned, it is primarily to change the conversation. To bring different perspectives, data, and experience together to create new outcomes. Once the right connections are in place, these high-value conversations have to be designed and enabled. Otherwise, the organization falls back on past habits.

For example, Accenture's legacy culture had powerful norms around performance and ownership of profitability. In fact, the past company tag line was *High Performance, Delivered*. A number of formal and informal systems worked together to drive these behavioral norms. No one succeeded in the company without meeting profitable growth objectives. The system resulted in tremendous growth but did not incentivize fully the collaboration across boundaries that is now needed to win in the 2020s. The accountability-at-all-costs orientation had produced tall silos and incentives for leaders to hit targets for their own entity while sometimes leaving money on the table that might have resulted from an end-to-end offering. For example, deep relationships in client IT functions were rarely leveraged into internal introductions for other c-suite functional engagements in the same company, which left the door open for competitors.

Conversations would have to be reset to yield collaborative decision-making at the market unit level, aligned with the center-led strategies of the industries, the services, and their individual practices. Each conversation would need to be redesigned by level to include the right roles, cadence, and decision guardrails. Critical conversations at Accenture include:

- client priority setting for the market unit, across industries and practices
- offering and campaign strategy and content
- business objective setting
- client solutioning, bundling the ingredients
- resourcing and staffing priorities
- market investment in talent, acquisitions, and new capabilities

The decision-making guardrails are foundational to changing the nature of conversations. After working with scores of companies on this challenge, we have learned a few things. Recall Romme's argument: the simpler the layers and rules of authority and hierarchy, the more likely individuals will self-organize to accomplish the goal by stepping up on the *responsibility* ladder. In the complex matrix this is a critical idea. It is impossible to parse authority into precise decision rights for every situation that a company such as Accenture must manage. As C K Prahalad points out, managers who seek "administrative clarity" simply cannot move fast enough in the horizontal organization. Leaders in the global matrix must learn to cope with decreasing degrees of strategic freedom while taking more initiative to act (Prahalad and Oosderveld, 1999). This initiative is enabled by practical and simple decision guardrails that create those strategic boundaries and provide freedom to make decisions within them.

The Right Leaders (and Leader Behaviors)

Accenture has been proactive in setting new expectations for leaders. Julie Sweet has been instinctive, with clear messaging to her top team. "Collaboration at scale" is her mantra, understanding that in a company the size of Accenture, this was going to mean new leadership teams. Once she had established the new executive committee (the strategic layer), she was purposeful in thinking about the integrative layer of leadership and chose to establish an extended leadership team of nearly 40 key leaders from all the major dimensions of the new organization. The new global management committee was convened prior to the announcements about the large-scale organization change. She engaged this new extended team in working through the details of the new design and assigned them oversight responsibility for the activation work that would take many months to complete.

A series of implementation conferences were scheduled January through March 2020 in a cascading fashion to engage the top 450 leaders. The culmination of the series was a multi-day launch program, conducted concurrently in North America, Europe, and Asia ahead of the March go-live date, portions of which were broadcast live across the locations, with satellite-enabled conversations among participants on the three continents. The program included a number of breakout workshops utilizing a set of real-world scenarios that captured the tensions members would face as they made decisions across the dimensions of the new organization. Collaborative leadership models, including a simple but effective trust framework for facilitating new conversations, were featured. Leaders practiced using these tools over the course of three days, and they shared reflections at the end of each day with video conferencing and pulse electronic surveying tools.

While the launch clearly communicated new expectations, the system to drive a new ethos of shared success across the company had to be adjusted to make these desired collaborative behaviors easy and rational. This system includes accountabilities, roles, priorities, individual and team metrics, performance management, and rewards. While the framework was set as part of the upfront design work, a big piece of activation is refining the many details over time. This interconnected system is essentially the management software that runs the company and, like software, has to be continually improved with user feedback. The work under way now is to ensure that the system that underpins shared success is understood deeply and can be brought to life by leaders in their everyday actions with colleagues and their teams.

Looking Ahead

Once the organization had settled in for 90 days, a survey was sent to over 600 leaders to assess what was unclear in the new organization model, how new conversations were going, and examples of trust building. The survey focused on the work and behaviors of leaders—both bright spots and gaps. The survey was used to diagnose progress. Where was there design work still to do, what was normal tension and confusion expected in making change in any global 500,000 employee system, and what was exacerbated by the Covid-19 pandemic? This last factor was not insignificant, as the growth model launch coincided with a global shut down. While Accenture transitioned flawlessly to virtual work, internally and with clients, the inability to meet in person took a toll on relationship building and the kind of problem solving and trust building that is so much easier when large groups are together.

Based on the survey findings and other data points, an activation plan of work was developed with an infrastructure to support it. A highly regarded senior executive was appointed as a full-time program manager to keep the work streams aligned, raise issues to the executive sponsors, and clear obstacles. This type of investment in activation infrastructure is essential to maintain the energy and focus this type of change requires over time.

Key Takeaways

- Activation is design-led organization change. It is the iterative process of learning and adjustment that takes place as leaders bring the new operating model to life.

- Activation goes beyond change management to ensure that the right connections, right conversations, and right behaviors are in place. It focuses on creating an interconnected system of accountabilities, management processes, decision rights, role clarity, priorities, metrics, and rewards that shape behavior in accordance with the strategy.

- Activation requires sustained commitment by leaders, who are in turn supported by an internal team that continues to work on a focused plan over time.

References

Kesler, G and Kates, A (2016) *Bridging Organization Design and Performance: Five ways to activate a global operating model*, John Wiley & Sons, Inc, New York

Prahalad, C K and Oosterveld, J P (1999) Transforming internal governance: The challenge for multinationals, *MIT Sloan Management Review*, Spring

INDEX

CPSIA information can be obtained
at www.ICGtesting.com
Printed in the USA
LVHW072134130323
741555LV00033B/997